THE HUMANITY OF CHRIST

THE
Humanity of Christ

Contributions to a Psychology of Jesus

BY

ROMANO GUARDINI

Translated from the German by
RONALD WALLS

PANTHEON BOOKS
A Division of Random House
NEW YORK

NIHIL OBSTAT   Joannes M. T. Barton, S.T.D., L.S.S.
                 Censor Deputatus

IMPRIMATUR ✠ Georgius L. Craven
                 Episcopus Sebastopolis
                 Vic. Cap.

WESTMONASTERII   Die 12a Septembris 1963

The *Nihil obstat* and *Imprimatur* are a declaration that
a book or pamphlet is considered to be free from doc-
trinal or moral error. It is not implied that those who have
granted the *Nihil obstat* and *Imprimatur* agree with the
contents, opinions, or statements expressed.

THIRD PRINTING

© Copyright, 1964, by Random House, Inc. and
Burns & Oates Ltd. All rights reserved under Inter-
national and Pan-American Copyright Conventions.
Published in New York by Pantheon Books, a division
of Random House, Inc., and simultaneously in Toronto,
Canada, by Random House of Canada, Limited.
Manufactured in the United States of America

Library of Congress catalog card number: 64-11806

Originally published in German as *Die Menschliche
Wirklichkeit Des Herrn*
     © 1958 by Werkbund-Verlag, Würzburg

TO THE MEMORY OF

KARL NEUNDÖRFER

CONTENTS

Chapter   *Page*

PREFACE   ix

I. THE SETTING AND THE LIFE   1

   1. The Historical Situation   1

   2. The Kind of Life   5

   3. The Basic Figure   17

II. ACTIONS, CHARACTERISTICS, ATTITUDES   32

   1. Introduction   32

   2. Jesus' Thought   33

   3. Jesus' Volition and Action   37

   4. Jesus and Material Things   42

   5. Jesus and Men   46

   6. Emotion in the Life of Jesus   51

   7. Jesus' Attitude towards Life and Death   53

III. THE PROBLEM OF THE STRUCTURE OF
PERSONALITY   61

   1. General Remarks   61

   2. The Structures of Growth   62

   3. Temperament and Behaviour
     Structures   76

   4. Jesus Is Unique   80

IV. JESUS' MODE OF EXISTENCE 90

    1. The Person and Existence of Jesus 90

    2. His Achievement 97

V. THE UTTER OTHERNESS OF JESUS 101

    1. The Absolute Otherness Affirmed 101

    2. Jesus' Originality 111

    3. Jesus' Being Come 126

    4. Jesus as Teacher, as Power, as He
       Who Is 136

PREFACE

I

THIS book is an essay gathering together the results of many years of study. While the problems treated here would certainly seem to require still further elucidation, their manifest timeliness leads me to follow the suggestions of friends and publisher and to present this essay as it stands, in the hope that further discussion may benefit thereby. The work goes out now in the shape it acquired about ten years ago as a series of lectures.

I should not like to put forth this book, however, without first mentioning how the problems have been approached, and how they relate to the general picture of theological thought in our time.

We view with mixed feelings the pre-eminence which the science of psychology claims in our day. The procedures of observation and analysis seem to intrude into every sphere of life. They choose above all to focus on the structure of personality, not excluding—indeed rather preferring—the structure of those personalities we call great. While the achievements, no doubt, merit attention, we must bear in mind that both the methods and the results of psychological research are determined, even more than are those of other sciences, by the motives which lie behind them. We have, therefore, every right to be sceptical, for these motives, whether acknowledged, half acknowledged, or unacknowledged, are multifarious and frequently quite unacceptable.

Psychological analysis may well be motivated by the desire to improve our understanding of the nature and destiny of some personality and to assess it more accurately—to give it, that is, the honour due to it. It may, however, just as well spring from the will to insert both personality and man as such in a merely natural context, thus confounding him with an order inferior to him. Were that effort to achieve its aim, the result would be a triumph at the cost of reverence.

Motives of both kinds have always exerted their influence and are doing so today. Those of the second kind, however, have been greatly strengthened by certain contemporary trends. Democracy of the truly radical sort will not tolerate gradations of rank among men. Positivism and materialism both deny any essential difference between the spiritual and the animal, between man and beast. According to totalitarianism the business of science is not to discover what actuality is, but to change it and make it what it should be. In practice this means placing men at the disposal of power. All this enables us to understand why those who care about human worth and dignity distrust psychology, especially in instances where what is at stake is the worth and dignity of a great man, and why they feel that some destructive force is at work, some technique of laying violent hands upon what has a claim to be reverenced.

Inestimably greater, then, are the misgivings bound to arise when the subject of a psychological enquiry is none other than that One who not only surpasses all the great men of history but, indeed, completely transcends everything merely human—none other than Jesus Christ.

On the other hand, we must not forget that he called himself the Son of Man, a name which, all things considered, is much more than a mere term designating the Messiah, which he had taken over from the prophets. Jesus Christ is man, more unreservedly man than anyone else can ever be; for to realize human nature as he did was an achievement possible only for one who was more than mere man.

This point of view is in sharp contrast with the modern tendency to interpret man in terms of a lower order: to see in his present state a stage in an uninterrupted, steady ascent from the pre-human, and in his structure an admittedly more complex, but essentially identical, ordering of the same elements as in that of the animals. The contrary is true: man can be properly understood only in terms of what is above him. The final word on the meaning of the biblical text: "God created man in his own image" (Gen. 1. 27) was only spoken by "the Word made flesh" (John 1. 14).

Seen in this light, the problem of a psychology of Jesus appears to be one of the most urgent tasks confronting theology.

II

Early Christology sought, as its first task, to establish, beyond any shadow of doubt, that Jesus of Nazareth was more, and other, than a mere creature. Our minds, dulled by everything said and written on the subject, can no longer comprehend the passion with which for centuries the early Christians fought out the issues of Christology—a passion which can, in spite of its many all too human features, yet be called holy. In the end, the declaration affirming Christ to be the eternal, con-

substantial Son of the Father was established as a pillar
of truth never again to be shaken.

The second phase came when the Christian mind saw
clearly that this Son of God had truly become man in
Christ. It was not that he had come merely to dwell *in*
a man: he came as an actual member, indeed, as *the*
crucial and all-important member, in the whole history
of the human race. He was completely within human
history, yet at the same time quite independent of it.
Indeed, the very reason for the uniqueness, the redemptive force of his entry into human history, is to be
sought in the fact that he came from the freedom of him
who is above all history and above the whole world.
This is what he meant when he said, as St John reports:
"I have power to lay down [my life], and I have power
to take it up again" (John 10. 18).

Thus the divine rigour of this true incarnation had
to be purified from every notion which, while apparently affirming a maximum of incarnation, in fact
destroyed its reality, because it substituted for a personal event one which, in spite of the appearance of
sublimity, still remained at the natural level: namely,
the confusion of the natures. A being in whom the
human blended with the divine in a single, undif-
ferentiated substance would be a myth. And so arose
the concept of one person in two distinct natures, a concept which exceeds the capacity of the human mind, to
be sure, but which guarantees the integrity of the God-
Man.

The reality of the divine nature in Christ was now
unassailable, his true humanity was likewise established,
as was also the indissoluble unity of the two natures in
the person of the Logos: a unity which constituted the
basis for the historicity of Christianity, a unity which

we may perhaps even say made God himself historical. In saying this, we mean, of course, something very different from the pantheistic processes of the Absolute. And so, we now have these truths before us in a form which is both sublime in purity and rich in content, both truth and mystery together: they have become dogma.

And then the spirit began to ask further: what was the place in history of the Son of God made man. This led to attempts to merge the unique historicity of Jesus in the universal historicity of human life; and this resulted in all those images of Christ which represented him as sheer man—even though a most extraordinary man—or, on the other hand, as an idea, a myth, the content of an experience.

We know that these ways are wrong. Alerted by the attitude of the Church, theology is able to ward off all such attempts. But this resistance—if I interpret it correctly—has remained essentially negative. It has told us what is not. Now a positive task must be undertaken. We have seen how the existence of Christ proceeds from an event which resists any attempt to identify it with universal historical concepts. We have seen also that we cannot penetrate the heart of his personality, not merely empirically, because we lack the necessary means for such an insight, but in principle. For, to achieve this, we would have to be able to reduce the absolute reality of the divine nature and the relative reality of human nature to a common denominator—which is impossible.

But something else is possible: the fact can be brought home to us that the existence of Christ was a real earthly existence, taking place within the framework of actual history. He had his own inward and outward experiences, his encounters with men and things, his decisions and actions to be constantly taken and performed, and so forth. All this took place within the realm of being and event, that is to say, it can be understood. Hence the questions what, how, why, wherefore, whence and whither, can properly be asked and answered; and so also can the psychological questions, but—and it is an important but—they must be asked with regard to a fact which prescribes both an attitude and a method. This fact is the one already mentioned: the incomprehensibility for us of both the origin and the heart of Christ's personality.

So this psychology is going to be of a peculiar kind. If the word means, as it generally does, an analysis of personality and individual circumstance, then there can be no such thing as a psychology of Christ. The eternal decree that he was to become man, no less than the existence of the Logos in human flesh, resists any attempt to induce it to a psychological concept—or to an historical one, for that matter. On the other hand, the decision of the Logos to become man embraces everything that is essential to human nature, including the possibility of being understood. All the circumstances which determine human existence—body, soul, mind, society—attain their fulfilment in the being and life of Christ. Basing ourselves on these circumstances, we can, it is true, come to an understanding or, in other words, a psychology, but we are going to find that, owing to its inherent limitations, this psychology will be baffled at each line of approach towards precisely these circumstances which we try out. And, it must be repeated again, this defeat results not from any lack of material, from any dullness of insight or deficiency of method, but from the very nature of the object being investigated. The more complete the material, the more penetrating our insight, the more thorough our method, the clearer and more decisive becomes the impasse in the conviction forced upon us that our undertaking simply opens out on to the incomprehensibility of God incarnate.

III

How little justice was done to the figure of Christ by the historical and psychological method of the liberal school of theologians! The repercussions of this tendency in Catholicism, known as Modernism, have been overcome. We know not only that a watered-down version of Christianity is erroneous, but also that it is not even worth while wasting energy trying to provide it with an intellectual basis. The self-commitment of faith only makes sense when directed towards the one complete, unadulterated revelation with its suprarational appeal.

Yet, on the other hand, it is evident that Christology must go a step further. Not merely because of the logic of theological development, but for the sake of Christian life. Prayerful meditation requires an approach which will lead it deeper into the heart of real reality. The same thing is true of life and action as well. We are accustomed to think of the Christian life as a "following" or "imitation" of Christ. But what do we mean by that? In what sense are the person and life of Jesus normative for us? If we are to go any further than the usual abstract applications; if Christ's actions, sufferings, behaviour and attitude are to illumine and guide our human existence; if the idea of the "new man" who "is being changed into [the] likeness [of the glory of the Lord]" (2 Cor. 2. 18) is to acquire a definite, inspirational content, then this image must be made more concrete than is usually the case.[1]

This is the task, essentially, of a "theological psychology", the sort of thing I referred to in my short work on *The Mother of the Lord* (1955), and which I tried to provide, very tentatively, in my book, *The Lord* (1937).

In this connection, we may dwell for a moment on the phenomenon on which research might well try itself out and from which it could perhaps deduce many of the concepts it will need. This phenomenon is the saint and the life of his soul.

Hagiography has followed a course of development not unlike that of Christology. The history of the way it dealt with its subject shows that it first elaborated an abstract ideal of the supernatural, then created more individual but still typical figures, and only finally succeeded in grasping the concrete, historical person. The picture of the saint appears, at first, in the highly stylized form of the ikon, to become gradually more and more concrete and individual. In the process it runs the very real danger of having all its originality levelled out to accord with preconceived historical or psychological patterns, until we come to the final stage of treating sanctity as a pathological manifestation. At this point the work of destruction is complete.

If the saint is what the Church knows him to be, then his figure, too, contains a heart which defies all analysis: the "Christ in us" of which the Epistle to the Galatians speaks (2. 20). Now, this Christ does not exist as a

---

[1] It should be noted here that the literature of spirituality, which is too often neglected by systematic theology, has anticipated many of the insights in this matter. It would be useful, therefore, to investigate the writings of the Fathers, the masters of the spiritual life and the mystics, for the light they can shed on all this.

separate transcendent entity above the man, Augustine, for example, or as an alien body enveloped in some inaccessible depth of his soul; he penetrates his genuine humanity and historical life. Furthermore, Christ has become identified with the essential self of the man, so that the Pauline text: "It is no longer I who live, but Christ who lives in me", can be completed by another: "and now for the first time I really am becoming my true self". The basis for a psychology of sanctity is to be found in St Paul's thought on Christ's in-dwelling and the "emergence of the new man within the old"; but, as far as I know, this idea has not yet really been exploited. If we think of the saint in these terms, we learn, I think, much about the way we ought to view the reality which is Christ.

We can see St Francis of Assisi, for example, as he is revealed to us by the biographies of Thomas of Celano or Bonaventure. They greatly overstress the supernatural aspect of his character and the image they create remains remote from the world of men. Again, we can see him as Sabatier portrayed him. Here we have a concrete picture of his life, it is true, but the essence, the heart of the saint has vanished. This is because Christ has gone out of the picture too. For, along with Francis of Assisi, Christ also is classified as one of a series of individuals belonging to the same psychological type, that of the *homo religiosus*. This train of thought finally becomes lost in the rationalism and lyricism of a Henry Thode, Hermann Hesse, or Nikos Kazantzakis. We are today engaged in the task of penetrating to the true nature of Francis, who lived in the mystery of a likeness to Christ such as, perhaps, no other individual has ever achieved in such charismatic exactness. For that very reason he possessed so definite and so unique a human personality that he was able to influence history as few others have been able to.

IV

Finally, we must go into the question of method, for this sums up the whole difficulty. In view of the confusing variety of images of Christ current today, we must ask the further question: Which Christ have we in mind?

If we answer: The one who brought us the fullness of revelation and revealed himself therein, then another question must be posed: Where is he to be found? There is only one answer to this: In the New Testament. But this means, in the complete New Testament, in all its books, and from their first to their last sentence, and this brings us to the heart of the theological problem.

The reality of Christ has been made known to us by means of the words, i.e. the recollections, of the apostles, of all the apostles from Mark to John. But this does not mean that the genuineness of the figure Christ diminishes the further the witness is removed in time. The interval in time between Luke and Mark does not mean that the theologian must be wary of the later Gospel. It is even likely that the passage of time will have allowed the writer to gain a fresh insight into the nature of Christ. As a result of discipleship, prayer and meditation on his sayings and acts, a new experience of his reality will have been gained, so that when he proclaims Christ's message he will be able to say things which before were impossible or untimely.

When research comes back from St John's Gospel to an examination of the earlier ones, this does not mean that it discovers forthwith more authentic strata of the reality of Christ, but only ones that were perceived earlier. On the other hand, if, as we proceed from the earliest to the later statements about him, we find the emergence of strata in the picture of Christ which show evidence of riper reflection, greater metaphysical comprehension, and a more concrete appreciation in terms of contemporary problems, the message proclaimed does not become less genuine; but factors do emerge and impose themselves precisely because of the general situation and the stage reached in the progressive unfolding of the message.

Were we in a position to disregard all such accounts and gain an immediate impression of Jesus Christ as he was on earth, we would not be confronted by a "simple" historical Jesus, but by a figure of devastating greatness and incomprehensibility. Progress in the representation of the portrait of Christ does not mean that something was being added to what was proclaimed; it means that we are witnessing the unfolding step by step of that which "was from the beginning", on the supposition, of course—and this is fundamental—that as God willed the revelation of the redeeming truth of his eternal "Word" in Christ, so he also willed and brought it about that this truth should, in fact, be handed on to later generations;[1] and handed on in such a way that it could

[1] It passes understanding how any study of the biblical texts which does not take into account this supposition, but treats them like any other historical source, can merit the name of theology. Such an approach presupposes a vagueness about basic principles which is quite inadmissible in the realm of scientific thought. We have to do here, however, with a perversion of the idea of science which can be observed in other domains also. Science is the study of a subject by means of the method required by this subject, not by means of some generally applicable method which undermines its specific character.

be included in the simplicity of the act of faith, and
need no specialized knowledge to extract it from the text
of the Gospel message.

We have said that the source for our knowledge about
Christ is the memory of the apostles, of all the apostles
and throughout the whole time that they were proclaim-
ing the divine message right up to their death; that is,
from the day of Pentecost until the death of John. These
were no mere individual reporters, each one of whom
would be credited only to the extent of his personal
abilities. They spoke as apostles, that is, as "pillars" and
members of the Church. The Church, that is, the sum-
total of local communities, their faith, liturgical life,
prayer, etc., is not something existing alongside or apart
from them, so that it would be legitimate to make a
distinction between a valid original witness and a
secondary "theology of the community". The apostles
are themselves the Church. They are the Church in her
earliest kerygmatic phase, when she derives her commission and authority directly from Christ and the Pen-
tecostal enlightenment. This phase, as we have said,

Theology can be called a science precisely because it uses, not
the methods of general history or psychology, but the method
demanded by the nature of the object being investigated, which
in this case is revelation. This nature is not something purely
personal which the student subjectively attributes to his subject, and which then has to be discarded as soon as the investigation becomes scientific. Theology is rigorously scientific only
when it accepts the nature of revelation as the determining
factor in its choice of method. It is obvious that this consideration recognizes in the phenomenon a special complication, and
that the processes of research require a special competence in the
student's eye to enable him to identify unerringly his object,
and in the dialectic which will serve him in its conceptual
elaboration. Only to the extent in which theology fulfils these
conditions can it be regarded as truly scientific.

extends from the author of the first logion to the writer of the Apocalypse.

It is obviously pertinent to ask what kind of picture of Jesus they painted in the various historical stages of their preaching. A particular interest attaches to the question of the picture found in the very earliest preaching. The search for these strata, however, must not be dominated by a suspicion as to the validity of that preaching which would tend to assume that it became less and less reliable as the first century wore on. Our aim must not be to "get behind" the apostolic preaching in order to reach the authentic Jesus, thus freeing ourselves from too close a dependence on the "temporal limitations" of the apostolic message. The authentic Jesus is revealed to us by the apostles, by them alone, and by all of them together.

The attitude we are criticizing would be, not "scientific", but agnostic. It would amount to a volatilizing of the only specific object of theological investigation, and, consequently, of the whole scientific character of theology. The different ways in which Paul, as compared with Mark, and John contrasted with Matthew, recount the Gospel message are an element of their apostolic mission. The fact that they were impelled (or enabled) to fulfil their task by the changed circumstances of the later period in which they lived and worked is due just as much to the Spirit of Christ as was their enlightenment at Pentecost. So the picture of Christ which is transmitted by the later preaching of the apostles is as authoritative for the reality of Christ and as much an object of faith as is the content of the earliest preaching. By the same title, it constitutes, as readily as the former, the valid object of theology as a science.

The attitude described earlier also closes its eyes to

the full reality of Christ in terms of method. It begins
with the assumption that the first, "historical" Jesus was
the "simple", unmetaphysical, purely human individual, and that his true greatness lay in his human
genius, the depth of his religious experience, and the
power of his teaching. Thereafter, it is affirmed, this
primitive reality was metaphysically inflated in the
course of the first century, was assimilated to the
mythical category of the "Saviour" and adapted to suit
the religious needs of the communities which felt the
need of a cult figure. To admit this is to abandon at the
outset everything that could merit the name of "revelation" in the true sense of the term, namely, the communication of a reality not conditioned by man, but
sent to him from God in order to judge and redeem all
mankind. At the same time, it abandons at once everything which the passage of time, the increasing remote-
ness from the original event, the development in historical circumstances, and the tradition that welds all
that together, can contribute to a disclosure of the
"beginning" of that Reality which is the foundation of
redemption and the controlling force of history. To
repeat : the contrary of that premise is true. If we could
get back to the "original", that is, if we could work our
way back to the picture of Christ as it existed before it
had been turned over in the apostles' minds or
elaborated by their preaching, before it had been assimilated by the corporate life of the faithful, we could find
a figure of Christ even more colossal and incomprehensible than any conveyed by even the most daring statements of St Paul or St John.

The Christ who interests the scholarly theologian and
the faithful Christian alike is the figure which comes to
us from the whole of the apostolic preaching. And this

is so, not because that preaching is concerned with the "Christ of faith" as distinct from the "Christ of history", for that would mean that the Christ of faith existed only by virtue of a religious attitude towards him and was not existent and real by himself. Later accounts would then be nothing more than idealized versions of the various experiences of Christ; evidence of the various ways in which the apostles and their hearers had seen him in the course of the first century, preliminary drafts for the way in which the faithful of later generations would view him.

To make sense we must see things the other way around. The Christ whom serious believers believe in is the original reality. The statements of the apostles are guides to him which never quite do justice to the fullness of his divine-human nature. The apostles never state more about the historical Jesus than he actually was; it is always less. Consequently, everyone who reads the New Testament aright feels that every sentence is pregnant with meaning regarding a reality which surpasses all that is said about it.

As opposed to the rationalist approach, true biblical theology must now accomplish a kind of "Copernican revolution". Its scientific purpose must not be to isolate from supposedly over-emphasizing representations, as likewise supposedly simple original reality; its object must be to bring out clearly all the elemental greatness of the original, on the basis of a whole series of representations, all of which are valid, but all of which, in spite of a gradual deepening of perception somehow fall short.

It is this elemental greatness of the original which has been at work in history, has built up the Church, and has furnished the irrepressible impulse towards activity and transformation, which is a matter of past as well as present experience. This is what "is, and was, and shall be". This is the only source of salvation.

This is the Jesus Christ we intend to study in this work. The psychology of which we are speaking here is no kind of analysis of a merely human personality who was an initiator, for there never was such an individual. Rather does it try to understand the figure which emerges from the whole apostolic preaching of the first century and which in each phase of its proclamation points back to an original reality which towers above them all.

We are perfectly aware that both the object and the method of our undertaking will be called "dogmatic", in a derogatory sense, by that theology which calls itself "critical"; that this school considers such a subject matter to be chimerical and its method unscientific. In fact, however, the attitude of this school is based upon a false premise, namely, that the person of Jesus and its historical witness must be treated in exactly the same way as any other historical phenomenon.

True theology must open its eyes to that peculiar taboo of recent times, the spirit or principle of "scientism", which claims to be universally applicable, but in fact belongs to the spheres of the natural sciences and history, and which, even in those spheres, has assumed a purely positive and quantitative character. There has been a widespread inclination for theology to accept this limitation, and as a result much harm has been done. It is high time theology freed itself from this influence and appealed to standards consistent with its own nature. We need hardly add that this does not mean that we are underestimating or ruling out any of the exacting demands of philology or history.

THE HUMANITY OF CHRIST

I

THE SETTING AND THE LIFE

1. THE HISTORICAL SITUATION

ALMOST everything we know about Jesus comes from the New Testament, above all from the Gospels. These are not historical narratives in the modern sense. They do not even set out to provide edifying biographies written according to a unified scheme. They are a *holy message.*

Without attempting to achieve sequence and completeness, they record events, sayings, and actions in the life of our Lord, presenting them according to their significance for the proclamation of the message of salvation. Thus, from the standpoint of historical biography, the facts which we learn from the Gospels about the life of Jesus are at once accidental and precious.

The scene of Jesus' life is Palestine. Because in the later and more important part of his life he moved about with considerable freedom, the story takes us to widely different regions. First there is the immediate home-country—Galilee; then the capital with the surrounding province of Judaea; the solitude of the wilderness and the banks of Jordan; Samaria and the Syrian frontier. It is true that the account shows no interest in things which are not immediately connected with the holy message of salvation, and yet it throws light now and again upon the conditions of the country; upon the

peculiarities of the different regions with the tensions
which exist between them; upon occasional geographi-
cal and historical points of interest.

The time limits of Jesus' life are determined by certain statements in the Gospels. He was born during the
reign of Augustus Caesar, Quirinius being governor in
Syria, and Herod, the King of Galilee, under Roman
vassalage. We cannot fix the year exactly (Luke 2. 1–2;
Mat. 2. 1). His public activity began after the fifteenth
year of the reign of Tiberius Caesar, i.e. after the year
28; for it was in this year that John the Baptist began to
preach, and Jesus appeared after that. Jesus was then
about thirty years old (Luke 3. 1–3, 23). He died, at the
latest, before Easter of the year 35, for his death
occurred while Pontius Pilate was in office, and by
Easter 36 Pilate's term was over (Mat. 27. 11–26 *et par.*).
Jesus lived, then, between these extreme dates. More
exact dating depends upon how long we allow for the
Baptist's and his own ministries, and how we interpret
the statements of the various Gospels concerning his
journeyings to Jerusalem. The highest reckoning puts
the duration of Jesus' public life at about three years;
the lowest at a little over one.

The reigns of Caesar Augustus (29 B.C.–14 A.D.) and
Tiberius Caesar (A.D. 14–37) form the historical framework of our Lord's life. All the world, from Gibraltar to
Mesopotamia, from Britain to Ethiopia, was a single
political entity. A multiplicity of local cultures was held
together by strong unifying forces, above all by a view
of life which blended Hellenistic intellectualism with
Roman practicality. Greek and Latin were spoken
everywhere. Political ordinances, a uniform administra-
tion, and commercial intercourse guaranteed a constant
interchange between the different parts of the Empire.

The religious scene presents a vast diversity; but the separate pagan cults had long since lost their sharp dividing lines. All of them had become imbued with certain tendencies, notably a predilection for myths and mysteries. A deep longing for redemption was felt everywhere, and this led to all kinds of syncretism.

The rulers of Palestine were the sons and heirs of Herod the Great (d. 4 B.C.). Judaea and Samaria were ruled by Archelaus (4 B.C.–6 A.D.) until his banishment, when Judaea was made a Roman proconsulate under Quirinius. Herod Antipas (4 B.C.–39 A.D.) ruled in Galilee and Peraea. Philip (4 B.C.–34 A.D.) ruled in the North-east, but his area, too, was destined to come under immediate Roman rule. The country's political independence, won by the Maccabees in the wars of freedom (167–142 B.C.), and upheld by the Hasmonaean dynasty, had been brought to an end by Pompey. From 63 B.C. onwards Palestine was a Roman province. Herod the Great himself had been a Roman vassal.

Despite this political dependence, however, a considerable spiritual independence persisted. The form of government was still the old theocracy, exercised by the high priest assisted by the supreme council of the Sanhedrin, composed of seventy-one members.

Supreme jurisdiction in matters involving the death sentence and crimes of a political nature was reserved to the Roman governor, as was taxation. Religious life was founded on a tradition which had withstood all change.

At the same time, a whole series of Greek and Asiatic influences had made themselves felt. The danger of hellenization may well have been warded off by the Maccabean wars and the country safeguarded for Judaism; but Palestine, too, was affected by Hellenistic culture, as well as by a religious movement which stirred the whole Mediterranean world, revealing itself in Palestine principally as a fervent longing for the Messiah, an expectation which was not purely religious but also strongly nationalist and political in tone.

The guardians of the nationalist-conservative tradition were the Pharisees. They were the *purists*, those who remained faithful to the Law. They were vigorously against all that was foreign and pagan; and they were the bitterest opponents of Hellenistic culture. And yet, for all their national consciousness, they were not really in touch with the people, but looked down on them as a despicable, confused, and ignorant rabble.

Opposed to them was the party of the Sadducees who were cosmopolitan and supported Hellenistic culture, seeing themselves as the enlightened, rationalist opponents of all that claimed to be above the senses or beyond this world.

Their image merges with that of the Hellenizers, the group that adapted traditional Jewish ideas to the popular philosophy of the times, and whose attitude to the Law was determined by this adaptation. The Sadducees were related also to the Herodians—members of the courts of Herod's heirs, who had no interest in serious issues but sought only power and pleasure.

A number of other well-defined groups stood out from the mass of the population.

Most conspicuous were the Essenes, a sect of a decidedly mystical and ascetic character.

John the Baptist's disciples seem to have had much in common with these people and while some of them adopted their master's attitude to Jesus, others continued as a separate community.

Besides these, we must take note of that little band that remained firmly within the ancient tradition, but drew its inspiration rather from the Prophets and the Psalms than from the Law. These were men and women of deep, quiet spirituality like Zachary and Elizabeth, the parents of John the Baptist; or the two prophetic souls who greeted the Child Jesus in the Temple, Simeon and Anna; or the family at Bethany, Lazarus, Martha and Mary (John 11).

Finally, there were the Samaritans, a racially and religiously hybrid group, the descendants of colonists who had been transplanted there at the time of the Assyrian conquest. They tried to hold themselves aloof from both Jews and pagans, but were unable to do so because of the confusing forces all about them. They were despised by their Jewish neighbours.

2. THE KIND OF LIFE

In this environment is set the figure of Jesus; here he lived out his life.

His ancestry is traced back to the ancient royal family, both in the genealogies and in isolated remarks (Mat. 1. 1 ff.; Luke 3. 23 ff.). This royal line had now lost all its power, possessions and significance, so that this late descendant lived in complete obscurity.

He grew up, not in true poverty, but in humble circumstances nevertheless, in the house of a simple craftsman—a carpenter. Jesus' general behaviour bears witness to the fact that he was accustomed to great simplicity, though we must not forget that he feels quite at ease among well-to-do people, and shows, for example, what he thought of the behaviour of Simon the Phari-

see, who had invited him but did not think it necessary to extend him the least token of hospitality (Luke
7. 44 ff.).

We do not hear of his having had any special intellectual training. The puzzlement expressed on several
occasions over where he got his knowledge of the Scriptures and his wisdom shows that he cannot have had
any formal education (Mat. 13. 54; Mark 1. 22; Luke
2. 47; John 7. 15).

Jesus' way of life is that of an itinerant religious
teacher. He goes from place to place as outward occasion
—a festival pilgrimage—or spiritual necessity—his
"hour"—demands. He often stays in one place for quite
some time, visiting the surrounding district and then
coming back to it again. Thus, for example, at the start of
his ministry, at Capharnaum (Mat. 8. 5 and 9. 35), or at
its end, in Bethany (Mat. 21. 17–18; 26. 6). This pattern
of life derived from the nature of his mission, not from
a personal wanderlust. We can deduce this from the
answer he made to the scribe who said he would follow
him: "Foxes have holes, and birds of the air have nests:
but the Son of man has nowhere to lay his head" (Mat.
8. 20). From his audience he gathered around himself a
band of the more receptive whom he instructed in the
deeper meaning of his message. From among these,
again, he made another selection of the Twelve. The importance of this selection is underscored by the fact that
the chosen are mentioned by name (Mark 3. 14 ff. *et
par.*); and it is also recorded that he spent the previous
night in prayer (Luke 6. 12).

The small inner circle, called "the Twelve" for short
(Luke 8. 1, etc.), are especially close to him. We may recall the intimate bond which existed in ancient times
between the philosopher or religious teacher and his

disciples. The Twelve are always about him. Wherever
he is invited, they go too. He shares food and lodging
with them. After he has spoken they cluster around en-
quiring into the meaning of what he has said. And he
tells them expressly that all is made clear to them,
whereas the multitude will have to be content with
parables (Mat. 13. 11 ff.). He sends them out to test
their strength; he tells them what to preach, what to
take with them, and how to conduct themselves on their
journey; and he gives them power to perform signs. On
their return he calls for their report, and the whole
scene reveals how deeply he was involved in their
activities (Mark 6. 7–13, 30–1; and cf. Mat. 10–11. 6,
25–9; Luke 10. 1–22).

Within the band of the Twelve there is a more select
group still, consisting of the Three: Peter, James and
John. They are present on all important occasions, such
as the raising of Jairus' daughter, the transfiguration on
the mountain, and at Gethsemane (Mark 5. 37; 9. 2;
14. 33). There was a specially close link between John
and his Master, so close in fact that he was able to describe himself as the disciple "whom Jesus loved" (John
13. 23; 19. 26).

A number of women can be discerned within the
wider circle of disciples. They are those whom he has
helped in bodily or spiritual ills, or who have attached
themselves to him for religious reasons (Mat. 27. 55–6;
Mark 16. 1; Luke 8. 1–2). Some are well-to-do and look
after his material needs.

St John's remark that one of the Twelve, Judas
Iscariot, kept the common purse (John 12. 6), answers
the question: What did Jesus and his companions live
on? Each member of the group no doubt contributed

something to the common upkeep; but in addition, those who were impressed by the Master's message helped out as well. We learn, too, that alms were dispensed from the common purse (John 13. 29).

Besides this we learn that Jesus had friends with whom he could stay. Considering his manner of life and the highly developed hospitality of the East, this was only natural. He had especially close ties with the household of Lazarus, Martha and Mary of Bethany (Luke 10. 38 ff.; John 11).

A characteristic element in Jesus' circle is constituted by the "publicans and sinners", people ostracized by the accepted standards of society because of their way of life. With him, however, they find understanding and love, and they, in turn, are especially devoted to him. His association with them, however, caused the shadow of suspicion to fall on him in the eyes of the devotees of the Law and of respectable citizens (Mat. 9. 9 ff.; 11. 19; 21. 31; etc.).

We now approach the question: What attitude did the various strata of society and groups in the land adopt towards him?

It was the common people who from the first responded enthusiastically to his person and his message. They could see that he did not speak "like their scribes" —formally, technically, incomprehensibly—but with vitality, from observation and experience; not theoretically, but "as one having power", so that they felt the dynamic power of his words and the mysterious Reality which lay behind the words (Mat. 7. 28–9; Luke 4. 32). They sensed also that his attitude to them was different from that of the members of the influential classes. In the eyes of the Sadducees, they were just a rabble; to the Pharisees, they were the despised masses who "do not know the Law" (John 7. 49). By contrast, the attitude of Jesus made them feel that his concern for them was genuine. Words like those of the Beatitudes in the Sermon on the Mount have a primarily religious meaning. But they were in marked contrast to the standards of the wealthy, the powerful and the educated, and were therefore interpreted by the people as signs of sympathy for the distressed, the oppressed and the ignorant. This feeling was strengthened by the fact that Jesus was always ready to help the poor, the suffering and the outcast. Sayings like "Come to me, all who labour and are heavy-laden, and I will give you rest" (Mat. 11. 28) have reference first of all to his Messianic mission, but they also express his boundless readiness and power to be of service.

On the other hand, Jesus is no popular hero in the narrow sense of the word; certainly not in any sense of his being a champion of the lowly and simple against the wealthy and the educated. Certain sayings which seem to suggest this (Luke 6. 24 ff.; 16. 19 ff; Mat. 19. 23 ff.) in reality have nothing to do with social attitudes of this kind; still less do they imply any tactics of rousing the people against their rulers. In the same way, his relationship with the "publicans and sinners" does not mean that he is in revolt against law and morality, or that he favours moral decadence. His championing of the outcast is stressed because no one had ever done such a thing before. The reason for it lay not in any inner fellow-feeling but in the fact that "they that are in health, need not a physician, but they that are ill" (Mat. 9. 12); and because they, too, are "sons of Abraham" (Luke 19. 9). Jesus is moved by the spirit of One who knows that he is sent to every man, regardless of his condition. But once this has been made clear, it must also be admitted that Jesus has a special tenderness for the poor and the outcast. This flowed from the ultimate purpose behind his entire mission, which was to upset all systems based on the standards of the world, in order to proclaim the unknown God and his kingdom. The poor, the suffering, the outcast are, through their very existence, forces of discharge capable of shattering the established order.

Furthermore, he did not allow the people to draw too close to him, and withdrew when the approaches were too pressing. He knew that the religious motives which inspired such enthusiasm could be confused, shallow and earthly, and that they might cause his message, especially his message concerning the Kingdom of God and redemption, to be seen in a false light (John 2. 23 ff.; 6. 15 ff.).

Among the ruling classes, the Pharisees, who were in closest touch with public life and all its manifestations, paid immediate attention to him. At once they became suspicious and began to work against him. They sensed the thoroughgoing contrast between him and them in spirit and mentality, and in their attitudes towards God and man. He himself often treated them openly as adversaries. This is obvious everywhere, especially in the famous invectives (Mat. 12. 22 ff.; 15. 1 ff.; 22. 15 ff.; 23. 13 ff.; etc.). Yet, his struggle with them was not one of uncompromising opposition. He recognized their function (Mat. 23. 1–3), appeared before them too as their Messiah, and, whenever they showed a glimmer of understanding the truth, received them (John 3. 1 ff.).

For a long time the Sadducees took no notice of him. Only at the every end, when a crisis was imminent, did

they become sufficiently disturbed to join forces briefly
with their former despised enemies in a common action
against him (Mat. 22. 23 ff.; Acts 4. 1; 5. 17 ff.).

We read that Herod had heard of the new teacher
and taken an interest in him (Luke 9. 7–9)—besides, he
always had shown his interest in anything to do with
religion, e.g. in his dealings with John the Baptist
(Mark 6. 20 ff.). Then he became suspicious and Jesus
was informed of his intention to kill him, whereupon
Jesus indicated clearly enough what he thought of him
when he called him "this fox" (Luke 13. 31 ff.). Jesus
did not come into personal contact with him until the
trial, and then the meeting went badly enough (Luke
23. 6 ff.).

At first the **Roman** governor was completely unaware
of his existence. He, too, was first forced to concern himself with Jesus at his trial. John, with his customary eye
for involved human detail, has given us an impressive
account of their meeting (18. 28 ff.).

We still have to emphasize the peculiar sympathy
which Jesus showed for pagans. This was made clear,
for example, when he met the Roman centurion or the
Syro-Phoenician woman (Mat. 8. 5 ff.; Mark 7. 24 ff.);
likewise, in what he had to say on Tyre, Sidon and
Sodom (Mat. 11. 20 ff.). Even his behaviour towards
Pilate has a frankness unspoiled by any kind of pre-
judice.

The same is true of his attitude towards the half-
pagan Samaritans—as indicated by his parable of the
man who fell among thieves, or his story of the ten
lepers (Luke 10. 30 ff.; 17. 11 ff.), or his reprimand to
the two disciples who wanted to call down the venge-
ance of heaven upon the inhabitants of a village of
Samaria because they would not give hospitality to the

travellers. As this last instance shows, he certainly did not intend to reject the Samaritans (Luke 9. 51 ff.).

Something must now be said about his personal habits.

He had no fixed teaching centre either near the temple or in a rabbinical school, but moved about from place to place. We have already noted that this way of life was not a manifestation of wanderlust. The instructions he gave the disciples he sent out may safely be taken to reflect, with certain limitations, the kind of life he himself led and the experiences he had gained by it (Mat. 10. 5 ff.). He taught wherever opportunity arose —in the synagogues, where, moreover, every adult Jew had a right to speak (Mat. 4. 23, etc.); in the porticos and courts of the temple (Mat. 21. 21 ff.; 21. 21–24. 1); in market-place and street (Mat. 9. 9 ff.); in houses (Mark 7. 17); at the well where people came to draw water (John 4. 5 ff.); by the seashore (Mark 3. 9); on hill-slopes like the one that has given its name to the Sermon on the Mount (Mat. 5. 1 ff.); in the fields (Mat. 12. 1); in the "wilderness", that is, in uncultivated places (Mark 8. 4), and so on.

When he was invited to a meal, he accepted (John 2. 1 ff.) even though his host was not kindly disposed toward him (Luke 7. 36 ff.). He healed the sick wherever he encountered them, and also went to their homes (Mark 1. 29 ff.).

But then he would withdraw once more from the crowd, even from his disciples and nearest friends, to retreat into solitude. His public ministry began with a long fast and communing with God in the wilderness (Mat. 4. 1 ff.). Time and again it is recorded that he went off alone to pray (Mat. 14. 23). He did this particularly before important events like the choosing of the apostles (Luke 6. 12 ff.), the transfiguration (Luke 9. 18, 28), and at Gethsemane before his Passion (Mat. 26. 36 ff.).

In all matters relating to custom and ritual, in the first place, he conformed to the Law like everyone else.

At the same time, however, he definitely set himself above the Law. He did this not merely in the sense that he expounded the Law more intelligently and more spiritually than the fanatics, as we see in his clashes on various occasions over the law of the Sabbath (Mat. 12. 9 ff., etc.), but radically. He looked upon the Law as something over which he had power: "The Son of man is lord of the sabbath" (Mat. 12. 8), and if Lord of the Sabbath, then Lord of the whole Law, of which the Sabbath was one of the most important parts. His anticipation of the Paschal meal by one day is likewise a sign of this lordship over the Law. At the Last Supper itself, this claim is made even more forcefully: not merely because he introduced into and instituted in this sacred rite himself, but because he annulled the rite itself and with it the whole old Covenant and announced the "new Covenant" and the new memorial feast (Luke 22. 20).

At this point we might ask about Jesus' outward appearance and manner. This is a difficult question to pose.

To ask what someone looked like, how he spoke or acted, is to presuppose a detachment which in fact we never find anywhere in the atmosphere which has surrounded the figure of Jesus for nearly two thousand years. When the question has been raised, however, as for example in connection with the various traditions concerning his true image, it seems to have had very minor importance. The question is also hard to put because the records, which are interested in quite other matters, make no direct comment on these details. They are concerned with Christ's importance in God's economy, his importance for the salvation of man. They concentrate on the absolute in his nature, compared with which all that is relative must yield. Thus, the image of Jesus has always been severely stylized. Any personal note we may discover is in each case attributable to an individual who has made it his interest. It will be found to reflect a particular kind of religious experience, or a special ideal of human perfection represented by some person or period as realized in the Redeemer. We need only point, in this connection, to the works of religious painters and poets.

So we shall not attempt to offer any solution, but will merely suggest where perhaps it might be found.

What sort of general impression does Jesus make if we compare him with the great figures by whom God revealed his will in the Old Testament, with Moses or Elias, for example?

The first thing which strikes us is his great calmness and meekness. We are apt to associate a certain weakness with these words. Was Jesus weak? Is he a figure of that tenderness which belongs to a late period in history when contrasted with the moods of earlier ages? Does he seem like some highly sensitive, vulnerable character of a later age, restricted by his very depth of understanding, so different from the creative and aggressive figures of early times? Is he merely the kind one, the all-compassionate one? Is he only the one who suffers and patiently accepts the burden of destiny and life?

Unfortunately art and literature have often presented

him in some such guise; but the truth is quite other-wise.

The impression which Jesus obviously made upon his contemporaries was that of some mysterious power. The accounts show that all who saw him were caught, and indeed shaken, by his nature. They felt that his words were full of power (Mat. 7. 29; Luke 4. 36). His actions —apart from special occasions—reveal a spiritual energy which marked itself off completely from all human standards, so that, when describing his nature, men turned to the familiar concept of the prophet (Mat. 16. 14; Luke 7. 16). But on occasion this energy burst forth in an overwhelming display of power, as in the episode with Peter after the miraculous catch of fish (Luke 5. 8), or during the storm on the lake (Mat. 8. 23 ff. *et par.*). There is not a trace of hesitant reflexion, sensitive reserve, diffidence, or passive spinelessness. He was filled with a power capable of any outburst or violence; but this power was controlled, nay trans-formed, by a moderation which took its source in his innermost being, by a deep goodness and kindness, and by a sublime freedom.

We could express the idea thus: Jesus is the personi-fication of a marvellously pure "humanity", not in spite of his enormous spiritual power, but precisely because of it.

This unity of power and humanity—taking the word in its purest sense—is one of the most prominent features of the figure of Jesus, especially as it emerges in the accounts of the first three Gospels. His will-power, his awareness of mission, his readiness to accept its consequences, and finally the mighty power of the Spirit—all this is translated into pure humanity so com-pletely and creatively, that we can describe his significance by saying: He is able to bring men to understand and put into effect what is meant by true humanity, even though—or *because*—he is more than a mere man.

To put it another way: unobtrusiveness is of the very essence of the "happening" we call Jesus.

We have only to compare his outward activity with other biblical or non-biblical happenings to see how the mighty word, bold gesture, powerful deed, fantastic situation, and the like, are alien to him. Strange as it may seem, the character of the extraordinary is missing even in his miracles. These are certainly great; many of them, like raising the dead, feeding the multitude, or walking on water, are tremendously impressive. But even these have something about them which makes them seem, one might almost say, "natural". This "humanity" of which we spoke reappears as unobtrusiveness.

Jesus' manner must have been very simple, his attitude so natural that people hardly noticed it. His actions proceeded quietly from the needs of the situation. There was nothing incredible about them. His words, too, had this unobtrusive quality about them. If we compare them with the words of an Isaiah, or a Paul, they strike us as being extremely moderate and brief. Compared with the sayings of a Buddha, they seem brief to the point of bluntness, and almost commonplace.

Admittedly, we receive this impression only if we think of his words in a purely philosophical, aesthetic or contemplative sense. If we consider them in the situation in which they were uttered and take them seriously, we then realize the power revealed in them, which goes far beyond "depth", "wisdom", or "sublimity": they touch the chords of existence itself.

3. THE BASIC FIGURE

The more a man reveals his uniqueness as an individual and the greater the influence he exerts on history, the more significant becomes the question: What is the basic figure on which his personality and his life are modelled? For over a thousand years the West has seen in the person of Jesus purely and simply the sole canon of perfection; and for a great part of mankind today that is still the situation. Even where this meaning is denied, the denial itself is affected by it. If we examine the attitude of Friedrich Nietzsche, for example—to cite only one of the most typical cases—we see that both the general scheme and special features of the picture of man which he paints are a contradiction of the conventional picture of Christ: *Zarathustra* is, in fact, an anti-Gospel figure. The same thing holds true of the war against Christian values in most sectors. Indeed, we might well ask if any view of man could be possible in Europe for a very long time yet, which was not coloured in some way by Christ. And so our question becomes all the more pertinent. To understand it better and to focus our thoughts on what is essential, let us first of all consider some lives which have come to be accepted as exemplary.

We shall begin with the man who has had more influence on determining the Western image of the "spiritual man" than almost any other person—Socrates.

Neither birth nor wealth was responsible for his fame. Intellectually, he was a product of self-training and of the most remarkable cultural milieu ever assembled in so small a space—the Athens of the fifth

century B.C. He was spurred on by an irrestrainable
longing for the truth; he had a powerful intellect and
an extraordinarily keen critical faculty. In addition, he
had a great influence on younger men, which was felt
by his followers to be something uncanny. He was a
religious man, with an unquestioning consciousness of
being led by God. While he tried to replace traditional
mythical notions by a system of contemplation enlightened by philosophy, he nevertheless retained such
a profound feeling for the mystery of things that he did
not openly rebel against his environment, but remained
faithful to its beliefs.

In this way, he lived a long life devoted to philosophical research and inquiry, a life spent in awakening
and training men's intellects. This activity sprang from
his own inner nature; it also took on the consecration of
a divine commission, for, as he acknowledged at the end
of his life before the supreme court, he knew that he
had been called to such a life by Apollo, the god of
light and mind. Moreover, this mission bore fruit. He
could see its good effects all around him. In the constant
struggle with his adversaries he displayed his own
superiority and he could rest assured that the future
would belong to him. He was surrounded by a host of
disciples, one of whom was Plato, a man of genius, to
whom he had imparted the best of his knowledge over
a period of ten years. Finally, the inner logic of his vocation led him to take his ultimate decision. At the age of
seventy, surrounded by his close friends, he died; and
the manner of his death set round his being and his
work a final halo of unsullied light.

The figure of Socrates can be compared with that of
another personality, also from Greece, who belongs, not

to history, but to legend. Nonetheless, he expresses very clearly that elemental zest for life that is so typical not only of the Greek but of universal man. The figure we have in mind is Achilles.

Achilles was no thinker; he was a man of action—handsome, fearless, passionate, skilled in all warlike pursuits and filled with a consuming desire for glory.

He had once been asked whether he would prefer a long, but uneventful life, or a short life which would make him the greatest in the hall of fame. He chose the latter. His life was thus a blazing flame soon extinguished; but for that very reason it was glorious, a symbol of that beauty which comes to flower, not through plodding enterprise and care, not through labour and endurance, not in any wide-stretching, fully traced arcs of life, but all in the extravagance and transience of youth. As Homer depicts him—the poet whom the Greeks regarded as more than a mere poet, rather as a teacher of things divine and human—Achilles was the very expression and personification of this zest for life.

The life of a Socrates or an Achilles proceeds directly from its own deep point of origin and fulfils itself with a necessity which is at the same time freedom, according to the law of its own nature. Everything that influences it from without has to serve the creative purpose dictated by the inner image. In contrast to this pattern we must cite another type of existence belonging to the antipodes, as it were, of ancient life—Epictetus, or, more precisely, the man whom Epictetus regards as a model, that is, the Stoic.

Both Socrates and Achilles experienced existence as something bound up with their own inner nature as something familiar. And so events and influences which affected them neither introduced any alien elements nor distorted the shape of their personalities as they unfolded. With the Stoic, on the other hand, things are radically different. He is neither venturesome nor an extrovert, neither borne along by a powerful urge nor protected by a hard shell. He tends to be a contemplative, and certainly has a sensitive and vulnerable nature. The processes of history, his fate, strike him as alien, even hostile, and he has the greatest difficulty in coming to terms with them. And so he retreats within the shell of his own nature, there to become master of his fate, or at least to learn how to put up with it.

He does this, indeed, by saying that fundamentally nothing affects him at all. This results in his thrusting his deepest self so far into the background that not only outward events but even his own individual nature, which is subject to change and decay, appear as something alien. He says not only to fate, to possessions, family, power and honour, but even to health, state of mind and basic endowments: "I am none of these . . ." What remains as his ultimate true nature can scarcely be called an "image"; it is more like a mathematical point, the focal centre of his being, a completely colourless self, invulnerable and indestructible. Everything that happens to it is regarded as mere occurrence, as something completely alien, something emerging from the realm of the unknown, uninvited and meaningless, and with which one's true nature must not be allowed to come in contact. For the Stoic, the basic process of human life is not unfolding, but affirmation and conservation. It is true that, involuntarily, a genuine figure is produced by this very process; a grim and solitary form, outwardly calm, but ablaze inside with hidden passion, desperately courageous and virile to the point of madness.

Between the extremes of pure self-development in a context of related contingencies on the one hand, and sheer self-assertion in the face of a hostile world on the other, we have the attitude which Virgil describes so well in his picture of Aeneas. Here, fate is what determines the content and meaning of personal existence.

Aeneas' ancestral home, Troy, was destroyed, a frightful disaster of which he felt all the horror and pain. But at the same time he received the assurance that, in spite of, or rather out of, this misfortune, he was being called to found a new city and inaugurate a new glorious period in history. And so he set out to face dangers and trials of every kind; not—like Odysseus—to roam the world and taste its marvels, but to find the spot where, according to divine decree, the new race was to be founded. His life was that of a warrior, but his aim was not, like Achilles, to win a warrior's renown, but to reach the place where his destined task was to be fulfilled and the foundations laid for the future.

His personality had neither the creative power of a genius, nor the brilliance of a hero's swiftly consumed flame, nor the grim courage of the man who stands alone. It was narrow and restricted, but it was capable of feeling, kindly and brave, and had an inflexible power of perseverance and doggedness. What made up the life of Aeneas was not the self-expression of his inner nature or the challenge of the world's glory, in the form of discoveries or great deeds, but a divine vocation —*fate*, in the true sense of the word. That is why he was called "pious"; because he was capable of understanding and accepting the contingent as a divine command.

Aeneas was the mythical ancestor of the most realistic power in the ancient world, the Roman empire. The consummation of this was reached in Augustus, the first "emperor of the world".

Finally, to these figures from the Graeco-Roman world, we can add another from the Far East, a religious figure—perhaps the greatest of all time, and the only one who can seriously be mentioned along with Christ —namely Buddha.

Buddha is curiously impersonal. His being is marked neither by a creative, self-expressing urge, nor by daring deeds and the kind of activity which makes history. He was dominated by an inexorable logic. We might almost say that he was a law of being assumed into an inflexible will. If we disregard, for the moment, the question of the truth of his message, we get the impression that in his life the world reached transparency, not in the positive sense that the world's totality was being revealed, as in a microcosm, in a single human life, as in Shakespeare's plays for example, or—in a different manner— in Goethe's genius, but in the form of a discovery, a lifting of the veil. It became apparent that the world was pain, guilt and illusion. Its deepest law was uncovered so that it could be overcome—even abolished.

Buddha grew up as a king's son in a privileged position. His education was such as to make him the perfect prince: he did and enjoyed all that makes life worth living. Then one day he came upon those things that make a man think: old age, suffering and death. These made him realize how meaningless his former life had been. He therefore withdrew from everything and embarked upon the search for reality. He went through the whole course of ancient Indian yoga exercises, including this domain also in his universal quest, and found that these things, too, did not lead to freedom. Finally, he arrived at the knowledge that all existence is but an illusion arising out of the will to live, and thought that he had found a way by which to abolish or annihilate existence itself. This knowledge did not come to him from some encounter with external things, nor yet as a grace from on high, but was the final consequence of the fact that he is as he is and has done what he has done; that means that his present life is the result of countless previous incarnations. Thus Buddha closed the circle of knowledge. He gathered a group of disciples about him, taught them so that they would be able in their turn to hand on his doctrine, and organized their communal life. Then, when he had had time to regulate everything, he died at a ripe old age surrounded by his followers, a death that appeared as the perfect consummation of his life.

The essence of his being cannot, perhaps, be better characterized than in the three names constantly given him in the texts: the Vigilant, the Perfect, the Teacher of Gods and Men.

The personalities we have been describing are quite different from each other, but they have one thing in common: greatness. Where we are dealing with this category, terrible things may indeed befall a man—one has but to think of Atreus or Oedipus—but, nonetheless, his whole life is on the princely scale and shines bright, no matter what the horror. He may suffer humiliation like Hercules, but he will still wrestle his way through to triumph while still in this life. The stature of his life is measured by the standards of worth. He does not have to face everything possible, but only what is fitting. And if, as in the case of the Stoic, "every-

thing possible" can befall him, then it is regarded
simply as non-existent and is pushed aside by the inner
core of self. Even when things are at their worst the rule
of congruity still applies. Only one who is no true man,
who is at the mercy of the commonplace, a mere slave,
has to suffer anything incongruous.

But what about Jesus? We note simply that he himself
claimed unquestionably to be the one who was sent, the
bringer of salvation, the exemplar of the true life; that
Paul declared him to be the manifestation of God (2
Cor. 4. 4; Col. 1. 15; Heb. 1. 3), and John described him
as the Word made flesh, both meaning thereby that his
was the most meaningful and purposeful life that ever
was.

If ever a life was normative in character it was his.
What was the pattern of his life?

As we have said, Jesus was born the latter-day descendant of a once royal line. His birth, however,
brought him no privilege, power, property or education. It served only to emphasize the more his social
status as that of an impecunious artisan. In particular,
it was of no positive value to him later in life. He
neither relied upon it as a pretext to claim anything,
nor did he seek to restore its ancient power. Furthermore, it did not in any sense form a background to give
greater relief to a life of self-abnegation. And yet his
royal lineage was significant in the sense that because of
it Jesus is most intimately bound up with antecedent
sacred history; and its stored-up heritage of attitudes
and reactions were expressed in his life, chiefly, by
making his position ambiguous and causing his true
character to be mistaken.

The first thirty years of his life were spent in complete obscurity. All that we hear about them is the short episode of the pilgrimage to Jerusalem at the age of twelve, when he became for the first time subject to this obligation. The whole period is marked neither by deep study, significant encounters, nor great deeds. We hear nothing about any great religious events. The only historical event recorded is the pilgrimage; all the rest that we find in apocryphal sources is mere legend. All we can say is that he led the life everyone else in similar circumstances led.

Then his public ministry began. He preached that the kingdom of God had arrived and was clamouring for admittance. He preached the renewal of life in the Spirit; that a revolution in history through God's creative power was at hand, a revolution whose nature had been foreshadowed by the oracles of the prophets; but that everything depended upon acceptance of the message by the Chosen People. At first he was successful: the people, including many who were influential, turned to him. A band of disciples began to follow him, men who, humanly speaking, had nothing at all extraordinary about them. Soon, however, a serious crisis arose. His various opponents, formerly at loggerheads with each other, began to unite in a common front. He was accused on the basis of a complete misrepresentation of the whole tenor of his teaching. The self-contradictory charge was made, on the one hand, that he was blasphemous; and, on the other, that he was preparing a revolt against Caesar. The trial was conducted in utter disregard of legal forms and ended in his condemnation. Certainly no more than three, possibly less than two, years after the start of his public ministry, he suffered death, an agonizing death, and of a kind to discredit him for all time.

The catastrophe was so complete that the crowd whom he had helped and who had shown such enthusiasm for him earlier, abandoned him, as did also a great many of his disciples. It was actually a member of the closer circle of the Twelve who betrayed him. At his arrest they all fled. The disciple whom he himself had called "the Rock" and regarded as the first of his followers, denied him—before a despised slave-girl of a portress, moreover, and even confirmed his denial by an oath.

After the death of Jesus, there occurred the event that broke all precedents, namely Easter. Humanly speaking, however, it in no wise made good the destruction of all his work. Though he had won through to glory and power, he did not seek to avenge himself on his adversaries, or crush those who had opposed him; nor did he triumph over those elements which had rejected him. The event simply served as a great turning-point in history: it was the starting-point for a whole new historical process which was to be set in operation at Pentecost.

Then at length, in the name of this figure and by the power of the Spirit, the final conquest of the whole world for God was set in motion.

How, now, can we characterize this life?

Was it the kind we have described as the unfolding of some great figure? Quite obviously it was not. What happened had nothing to do with any "unfolding": the concept is not appropriate. Nor did any "figure" emerge, to use the term in its proper sense. This concept is equally inappropriate. Nothing happened which in any sense opened up vistas of final "accomplishment". We witness, rather, a movement towards disintegration.

We have only to imagine what it would have been like had Jesus lived longer—fifty, seventy, or even ninety years! As things were, after the peaceful period of child-hood, youth and early manhood, there were left to him only three years or perhaps a little more than one year of activity and self-witness.

Was his death the climax of a life of heroic deeds? No; it had neither the character of a mighty assault against an overwhelmingly powerful foe, nor of a fire which consumes by its ardour a man's very substance. Still less was it a case of an over-generous spirit dashing itself in vain against the triviality of its environment. Christ knew and declared that the fulfilment of his goal was possible—but only through a free response on the part of those who were called: and the latter withdrew or even opposed him, not because he was asking more than the times could comprehend, but because they were unwilling to make a definite religious and moral commitment.

Can his life perhaps be regarded as an example of self-assertion amidst a storm of opposition? No, because what happened to him was totally at variance with the nature of the Son of God; many things, such as the story of the fish and the didrachma (Mat. 17. 23[24]–26), illustrate this. It was distressing, unworthy and incom-prehensible. The issue must not be allowed to become clouded as a result of the later significance which his life acquired. The cross has been placed upon the crowns of kings, but it was once a sign of death and ignominy. There were motives enough for adopting a stoic attitude; he did not do so. Jesus never made the slightest gesture of detaching himself from a hostile, de-grading, senseless world; of repelling what he could not avoid, as having no part in him, or of retreating within himself. What he had to contend with was wrong in every way, but he accepted it and, indeed, took it to heart, we might even say.

His attitude is one that had never been seen before, and one that cannot exist except where the norm of his person is accepted.

Aware that he had been sent by the Father, and filled with a desire to obey the Father's will in all things, he accepted everything that happened to him. We see in action a union with the will of God that drew everything that happened into the deepest intimacy of the love of God. By the very fact that everything became an expression—or, more precisely, an instrument—of this love, earthly things acquired for God himself a meaning of which no myth had ever dreamt.

What of the kind of life exemplified by a man like Aeneas, who felt that a divine commission was being fulfilled in a long life of patient suffering and struggle, and that life was a blend of adventure and action determined by that mission? This type is not that of our picture either. From the point of view of the ultimate goal to be reached, the events in the life of Jesus were not in the least necessary. His goal could have been achieved equally well—and from the viewpoint of worldly considerations, much more logically—by other means. True, Jesus was charged with a mission of utmost importance, but what were its terms of reference? In the last analysis, all we can say is that he was to come among men and enter our historical world as the One sent from God, to take upon himself the burden not only of his personal existence, but of existence itself, and live it out with a transparency of knowledge and a depth of feeling which could have no other source than this mission received from his Father. He was to set reality in motion and thus release all the potentialities inherent in it. He was to bear the consequences of his incarnation and thereby create a new starting-point for existence. In the final analysis, it would not be of great importance what actually did happen, so long as it was the proper thing required by the situation at that precise moment.

We could turn the statement round and say that, no matter how much blame attaches to those who caused Jesus to suffer what he did, for Jesus himself it was the right thing, ordained by God and, therefore, eternally right. Jesus himself expressed the matter in this way: Woe to them by whom offences come! Woe to those who create the conditions which lead to the misrepresentation! But for Jesus himself, "offence" is the very situation in which he must fulfil the Father's will. He expressed this idea by referring to his "hour". Jesus' life was not the expressing of a "personage"; he did not live according to some divinely constructed plan spread out before his eyes, but by the will of the Father as he encountered it at every step he took in going to meet his "hour". Those steps were not taken following a definite programme, but were, in each case, the result that followed from what had gone before and from the attitude taken up by the various people involved. Thus, union was achieved, at each stage, between the directing will of the Father and his own obedient will, and from this union his own actions followed.

As soon as Jesus' nature becomes clearer to us, we see that the category of "personality" does not fit him at all. Personality is a figure, in the sense of a man "modelled in the round" both as regards the basic structure of his nature and the actual course of his life: it is both the foundation and limitation of existence. Modern interpretations of Jesus have tended to turn him into a "personality", with the result that they completely lose sight of his most characteristic feature. He was something quite different. That is not to say that Jesus was a disintegrated person without either law of being or place in existence. This is not to say that he was a mere piece of flotsam to which anything could happen because his life had no distinct bearing of its own; mere human rubbish at the disposal of any power that tried to use it for its own purposes. It means, rather, that Jesus was clearly above and beyond any "figure". The various patterns of human life begin only on the hither side of his pattern of life.[1]

Granted that there is a logical thread running through the life of Jesus, it is one that is at variance with all accepted norms; one that makes manifest what is wholly "other"; one that reveals the mind and outlook of a religious reality so different from all worldly values that it proclaims itself precisely in its exploding of all worldly standards. The reality which it stands for is represented by the Beatitudes, or by the joy which Jesus felt when the apostles returned (Luke 10. 21 f.). To say this is, in the last analysis, only to repeat what has already been said, that the nature of Jesus was no ordinary "figure", in the accepted sense of the word.

[1] One might well ask if we have not in him, purely and simply, an example of the tragic figure of the prophet. This must be denied categorically. His figure was not like one of theirs. To begin with, it is striking that, unlike the Old Testament prophets, Jesus did not establish his authority by appealing to his calling. It is even more significant that he boldly claimed, unlike any of the prophets, to be the one model, rule, standard and way. Hence his mighty: "But I say unto you . . ." instead of the typically prophetic: "Thus saith the Lord."

Following the same line of thought, we may say that the life of Jesus is "Truth"; it is pure life without reservation or subterfuge; it is absolute harmony with the living reality of God. This identification with *Truth* was also an identification with the power of Truth and compelled those who encountered him to reveal their thoughts without reserve, to "disclose the secrets of the heart", as Simeon said at the presentation in the temple.

What can happen, then, in a human life which is determined by all this? The answer must be: Anything and everything. The question as to what can or cannot happen can never be answered by asking in turn what would be intrinsically great or small, proper or improper, constructive or destructive, fulfilling or frustrating. Everything can happen, even that which at first sight seems to be utterly inconsistent with holiness or divinity.

The reality of Jesus is of the kind which orders existence, literally conditions it, to reveal all its potentialities. For this reason it is not confined to one special form of existence, but is capable of appealing to every form, of entering every form, of transforming every form of existence.

II

ACTIONS, CHARACTERISTICS, ATTITUDES

1. INTRODUCTION

WHAT then are we to make of the psychology of Jesus? Having prepared the ground, we now ask this question aware of the difficulties involved. It is obvious that we are not concerned here with experimental psychology or the psychology of the conscious, or with any kind whatsoever of scientific analysis of the psychic processes as such, but with an attempt to understand, or to discover, the structure of the particular personality, to see how it works, how it acts, and, above all, what its inner motivating power is.

But even this is problematic when we are speaking about the person called Jesus. Psychology is embarrassingly inquisitive. It seeks to probe those things which the guardian-like inner personality prefers to keep hidden because they are sensitive and deserve respect. Psychology is indiscreet and tries to drag out into the open what modesty prefers to keep covered up because it may cause shame. A secret urge to destroy is at work in psychology and it knows that personality—a unique and inexplicable thing—is in danger of falling apart once it is translated into universal concepts and dissected.

This is true of every human person, especially of great and unusual figures. But there is a type of mentality which cannot abide the intellectual power and nobility of the great figure, and attempts to use psychology against it. This is specially true of this figure who affects so profoundly every man who encounters him. Psychology can be used as a means of destroying his claims. We need only recall the painful attempts to interpret Jesus as a pathological case. The scientific and literary works dealing with the psychology of Jesus in this vein should be a warning to us of the worst that can be done along these lines.

It need hardly be said, then, that our essay has nothing whatever in common with such tendencies. We are prepared to confront something which is greater than ourselves, and which, moreover, calls us to account, even though we may not be able to stand up to the test.

2. JESUS' THOUGHT

Let us begin with the psychic process most amenable to analytical treatment—namely, thinking.

How did Jesus think? Of what kind are the thoughts he expressed?

If we compare his thoughts with those of other religious leaders, they seem, for the most part, to be very simple, at least as expressed in the Synoptic Gospels. It is true that if we take the word "simple" to mean "easily penetrated" or "primitive", then this impression is dispelled on closer analysis. The thought of Jesus is neither analytical nor synthetic: it states basic facts; and states them in a way at once enlightening and confusing. Very seldom, and then for the most part only in St John, do his thoughts reach a metaphysical plane. Even then they do nothing more than state a plain fact. The only thing is that he happens to be speaking of the sublimity and hiddenness of the existence of God, speaking of the mystery of the Christian life. For the most part, the thought of Jesus, as expressed in his sayings, remains close to the immediate reality of things, of man and the latter's encounter with God. It is solidly realistic; but the realism is that of the man who is stripped bare by the judge of God and made new by his grace.

And so, Jesus speaks neither of the origin nor of the nature of the universe. He takes it for granted that the universe was created by God and finds its meaning in him; that it lies cradled in the hollow of his hand, and that he is guiding it towards a blessed future.

Nor does Jesus speak expressly about the nature of God. He presupposes what had been said about him in the revelation of the Old Testament, and passes on to its fulfilment by making known the way in which God is a *Person*, the way in which he can say "I" and "Thou" within himself. He does this, not speculatively in philosophical or theological language, but in a concrete way. He takes his stand within this divine life and speaks from it, as each successive occasion arises. Jesus spoke with greatest conviction about the Father, not revealing the ultimate mystery of this Fatherhood by explaining how we ought to think about it and how it is related to human fatherhood, but by telling us how this Father thinks and acts, and how man is to interpret God's Fatherhood seriously. Man will then achieve a real, existential encounter with God and come to the possession of the divine nature. His last word on the Father was said in the form of a prayer. A prayer is not doctrine but a guide to action. It exists, not to be thought about, but to be acted upon. If this is done, the worshipper

begins to understand more clearly the nature of the One
to whom he has turned.

Jesus was for ever speaking about Providence—again,
not speculatively but with direct reference to reality; so
much so that we are almost tempted to interpret his
words as the simple pious man's philosophy of life, or
even as a kind of beautiful childish fairy-tale (cf. the
image of the birds and flowers in Mat. 6. 26, 28). The
truth of the matter is that he presupposes the whole
Old Testament view of the relationship of God to the
world. It is a profoundly serious view and, for us today
especially, of far-reaching significance. Jesus totally dis-
regards questions about the possibility of God's providence, or about the precise relationship between the
existence of God and the course of world history. He
adopts a different approach: he provides us with a
guide to the workings of providence, telling us in the
Sermon on the Mount: "Seek ye therefore first the
kingdom of God and his justice; and all these things
shall be added unto you" (Mat. 6. 33). This is no
theoretical statement but a guide to the starting-point
for action, a signal to start off, and a promise that
strength will be given us on the way. And once a man
has committed himself, he soon discovers that he is
caught up in a process which demands nothing less than
the complete reorientation of his whole life. To the
extent that he does this, he achieves a true vision of
reality.

Much more could be said about Jesus' conception of
man, his moral teaching, and so on. Theoretical questions about the nature of existence play no part in his
thinking—as the latter is expressed in his words: what
lies beyond is unknown to us. It plays no part, not be-

cause it does not exist, but because Jesus' thoughts are oriented towards reality.

His thought was not intended to be a research course, a scheme, a mere intellectual construction or system, but to proclaim something which did not yet exist but was to come—namely, the kingdom of God. It pointed to a new reality and declared that it was meant for us. It made men cognizant of the fact that in view of this new reality events had been preparing which were now on the point of coming to pass. His thought is pre-speculative; but in a way different from the child or primitive man who has yet felt no need of facing the problem of truth in all its profundity. His thought is demonstrative, somewhat like that of the scientist who says: Here is a process in operation, something which has not yet been known, a possibility you have not yet grasped, powers which have not yet been at your command—be on the watch for them. Going deeper, we see the issue in another light as something still more fundamental. This reality can only be created by him, that is, by the Father through him. For example, the relationship of being a child of God is made possible solely because of the existence of Jesus. So then, he places himself at the very first movement in the creation of this relationship. His words are therefore authoritative in the fullest sense of the word. They are gift-bearing. Only because he lives, acts and speaks, does what he is speaking about exist. Only then can we begin to reflect about what has been discovered, about its nature and its relation to what we already knew, and so on. What he does is prior to all speculation because speculation is possible only as a result of what he does.

All this makes it quite clear that his thought eludes psychology. All we can say is that it is clear, concise, utterly responsible, with no trace of self or superfluity, concentrated solely on what is essential. He says—and says because he has brought it about: This is so. This is happening. Do this; power to do it has been given you. If you do this, things will turn out thus, and so on. There can be no "psychology" about this sort of thing, because it cannot be categorized. We are dealing with a revelation which is initiatory and creative and therefore incapable of being made an object of analysis. It is only from within this revelation, as for example about the manner in which it is experienced or effected, that some kind of analysis is possible.

3. JESUS' VOLITION AND ACTION

What about Jesus' willing and doing?

There are men whose interest is to know truth, to examine it thoroughly, and to explain it to others. Jesus was not one of these. He was concerned, as we have seen, with a reality that was not yet complete but was destined to be: with the reality of the sacred history of God and man; with the fulfilment of a divine decree and the consummation of an eternal destiny; with the coming of a new order of existence, that is, with willing and doing. But how did he will? How did he act?

It is not easy to answer these questions either. Once again our only way out is to make distinctions. Jesus did not exercise his will like a soldier making an attack; nor like an engineer drawing up his plans, weighing the possibilities, seeing and using all the means at his disposal; nor yet like a reformer with a guiding principle and a practical programme, or a workman who has his task and performs it step by step. And we must distinguish, too, when it comes to the means that he applied. Jesus did not use force by, for instance, gathering men around him and going ahead. He employed no hypnotism which, with his tremendous personality, he could easily have done. He did not operate by making promises of any sort, holding out the prospect of advantage in order to win agreement to his policy. He neither threatened nor bluffed. He appealed neither to appetite nor imagination. . . . How, then, did he will and act?

His will was of great power. It was perfectly at one with itself, without fear, prepared for anything that might happen, conscious that the stake was the one thing of supreme importance—the decisive moment for the whole of existence. It knew also that, in the absolute sense, the "time" had come. At the same time it was completely calm, unhurried, not to be pressed. And while his heart may have been filled with pain at the destruction of that infinite possibility, this did not affect his behaviour.

Jesus' will was in perfect union with the will of his Father who guides sacred history and fixes the appointed "hours" for things. The basic mystery of sacred history is this: God wills the coming of his kingdom and his will makes all things possible. But this will addresses itself to man's freedom and so can be rejected by man. As a result, the opportunity given only once can be missed; guilt and misery can arise, and yet all things remain encompassed by the will of God. This mystery permeated the volition of Jesus. He was aware of the infinite demands of the moment and did all he could to fulfil them. But the possibilities were measured not by human but by divine standards; and so there was no anxiety, no uneasiness, no excited activity. On the other hand, this resignation had nothing fatalistic about it.

What was wrong remained wrong, and the missed opportunity was not offered again. Yet appeal is made to a mystery which permits us to hope for all things, because in it love and almighty power are one and the same.

This will is firmly oriented towards its goal. It follows no programme that has to be carried out: what must be done at each moment arises of itself from the situation which develops at each step, depending upon the "hour which has come" (John 2. 4; 7. 30; 8. 20). This will is so compelling that Jesus says, in St John, that it is like hunger for the food which maintains life (4. 34). At the same time, he fully respects man's freedom. He never does it violence, by suggestion or inspiration, fear or surprise. The responsibility of the listener is always elicited and guided to the point where it must pronounce its own Yes or No.

Jesus was governed by a mighty, unerring, indomitable will, but he had neither "aims" nor "intentions". This will arose from no urge to create, dominate, reform; it was rooted in that reality of which we have spoken before. A work of God had come to maturity: "The kingdom of God is at hand" (Mark 1. 15). His will is to open up the road to this, but with the help of the truth of God which would be obscured by every act of mere human will, and with the help of man's freedom which would be compromised by any act of compulsion.

Will is inclined to isolate itself in its act of willing, to wrench reality away from truth and dominate it by force. No such thing happened with Jesus. His will was merely the obverse side of his knowledge, and his goal was truth alone.

Here, too, must be sought the source of Jesus' fear-lessness. This is not merely an expression of individual temperament. It does not mean that he had strong nerves, that he was cool-headed, resilient or enterprising; that he viewed danger as an intensification of life or felt himself to be carried along by fate. His fearlessness lay in his calm identification with reality.

He presented reality, this reality which is sacred truth, each time it was necessary, as the occasion demanded. He did so without fear, being himself hidden in that reality, because all that he desired was that reality, and he was ready to make any sacrifice for its sake. He did this, however, not like some enthusiast or fanatic who fails to see the consequences of his acts. He knew exactly what was going to happen. His courage came, rather, from the fact that in him will and truth were one, so that the greatest crisis which courage ever has to face, namely, when what is willed loses all meaning and the will sinks into the void, could never arise for him. He might suffer unimaginable torments; but the identity of his will with the meaning of it all, with truth, could never be destroyed.

What has been said thus far still does not enable us to understand the meaning of those words on the cross: "My God, my God, why hast thou forsaken me?" (Mat. 27. 46). To penetrate them we have to probe behind the question and ask in what sense he can be said to have felt the burden of responsibility for the guilt of the world on his shoulders and what relation that gives him to divine justice; but we cannot go into this here.[1]

We are now in a position to get some light on another question: Was Jesus well-advised in his behaviour?

---

[1] See below, pp. 74 ff.

In any case, we can affirm that he displayed no kind of mere cleverness. There is no trace of any kind of tactics, no playing one man off against another, no seizing an opportunity offered by a situation, no deliberately concealing some things while exaggerating others or making inferential remarks, or so forth. And this reveals something very significant about the elevation of his personality. Cleverness is proper in its place: but it does not seem to be a part of true greatness, especially in the spiritually-minded, and, above all, the religious man.

Jesus' way of life displays none of those methods which men employ to protect themselves in the battle for existence and to gain their ends, by pitting subtlety against strength, cunning against superior power, experience against great resources. In the sphere of Jesus' life there were no peripheral values, but always and only the one sacred issue, the "one thing necessary"— the glory of the Father and the salvation of the world.

Must we say, then, that Jesus' life was determined by noble and lofty ideals?

Offhand we would be inclined to answer Yes; but then we might begin to be assailed by doubt. These doubts certainly do not imply that there was in Jesus' life anything mediocre or base, any concession to weakness, cowardice or indolence, any departure from his absolute ideal. Even so, we cannot classify his character as noble or lofty in the sense in which we might apply these epithets to a hero or idealist.

For example, if "honour" is the strong, inexorable, yet sensitive and vulnerable thing which it is in the lives of men who are characterized by it; if it is a law which places men in a higher category than other men, but at the same time exposes them to the continual danger and probability, even, of total failure and disaster, then this is certainly not the determining factor in the life of Jesus, as his behaviour in its concluding phase shows. But this is not because he is found wanting in honour in any sense; it is because what is the decisive thing for him left honour far behind. There was indeed "honour" in his life; but it was his Father's honour, which gave rise to demands and entailed consequences which could not possibly be measured by the common view.

The same sort of thing is true of the values of greatness or graciousness or, indeed, any of the other aspects of *magnanimitas*. Closer analysis always proves that, in him, these values have not the importance they have in other personalities dominated by them. And this is because the thing which is decisive for him not only soars above the levels of this world, but confronts this world and its values, judges them, and reveals the new order of the unknown God, the "kingdom of God".

We cannot say, therefore, that lack of "prudence" or "cleverness" on the part of Jesus revealed the noble folly of the perfect hero. He had nothing in common either with Siegfried or with Parsifal; not because he was less than they in any sense at all—an average, drab personality—but because he lived at a depth which makes even these great luminaries appear somewhat immature. Compared with him their brilliance pales.

4. JESUS AND MATERIAL THINGS

What attitude did Jesus adopt towards material things?

Did he even notice them? Obviously he did. This is proved by his parables about the "lilies of the field"

(anemones), the birds of the air, the farmer and his kinship with the soil, the shepherd and his flock, the corn
and the threshing floor, bread, and salt, and lamps.
They also show that he was not indifferent to these
things. He understood and appreciated them.

We must, of course, discount the sentimentality of
legends and pious writers. In order to understand his
relation to material things we must go back to the Old
Testament views about God's creation. Things do not
constitute "nature" in the modern sense. They are
God's handiwork, and anything that happens is not
some spontaneous natural process but proceeds from the
power of God. Jesus was always referring to this creat-
ing and ruling God, completing the picture, however, by
presenting him as the Father, and showing that God's
activity was the work of the Father's Providence. This
thought explains his attitude towards things. To him
they were not merely scientific, poetic, or cultural data;
they were the materials and tools of Providence.

Not only was Jesus perfectly at ease with all things;
because his will was at one with his Father's, he felt himself to be Lord of all things. He was the one who had
been sent. His will was not for his personal interests; it
was devoted entirely to the purposes of his mission. And
so through obedience to this mission, "all power in
heaven and on earth" was given to him, a power as great
as that of the Father himself. This is a staggering
thought, but it is the view of Jesus. Yet this power is
never apart from or contrary to that of the Father: it is
always joined with it, in obedience to it. "My Father
worketh until now; and I work" (John 5. 17). The saying: "If you have faith as a grain of mustard seed, you
shall say to this mountain, Remove from hence hither,
and it shall remove" (Mat. 17. 20) is not a mere descrip-

tion of the limitless faith which his followers ought to have, but of his own faith too, only we cannot speak of his having "faith" in our sense of the word. He possesses, rather, that which evokes faith in us and makes it possible, namely, his essential identification with the truth and the will of the Father. That is why all things obey him.

When we look at his miracles in their true light, they reveal the peculiar contact in reality that the will of Jesus has with material things. This contact is not established through something in the way of "powers" of a higher order, but flows from obedience, from his union with the Father's will and the mighty course of sacred history, working itself out from hour to hour. At the point of contact between the exercise of the Father's power when he is forming the world that is to be, and the faith of men which links them with Providence, Christ is at work.

What value did things have for Jesus? What use were they to him? Did he enjoy them or prize them?

First of all, we must assert that he was not insensitive to the attraction of things. Had he been so, then an experience like that of the temptation in the wilderness (Mat. 4. 1 ff.) would not have made sense. "The kingdom of this world" could be used as a temptation only for someone who was aware of their "glory". Jesus was no ascetic. He said so himself in connection with John the Baptist's way of life. Jesus fully recognized this way of life; but he himself lived otherwise. Did they not even call him a "glutton and a wine-bibber" (Mat. 11. 19)? An account such as that of the marriage in Cana reveals anything but a contempt for things; and the same is true of the story, also in St John, of the anointing with precious oil at Bethany (John 2. 1 ff.; 12. 1 ff.).

On the other hand he himself mentions his lack of a home and possessions (Mat. 8. 20; 19. 21). Nowhere does he show any special interest in the value of things. Indeed, he warns us against the danger of this, especially in his sayings about the rich, in the parable about the needle's eye, and in the story about Lazarus the beggar.

We would, no doubt, be nearer the mark were we to say that he was completely detached from things, not as a result of self-discipline and a more spiritual view of things, but by nature. To him, things were simply there, part of his Father's world. He used them when it was necessary to do so, and took pleasure in them without making any special fuss over them.

Things represented no danger to him, as they do to men. But he does not demand of men that they should dispense with all things, as any ascetic or dualist system would. He asks men to free themselves from the thraldom of things. This idea is expressed most tellingly in the story of the rich young man (Mat. 19. 16 ff.). In answer to the question about what he should do in order to have eternal life, Jesus told him to keep the commandments, that is, to use things properly in obedience to the will of God; then all would be right. However, as soon as the desire to do even more is aroused, Jesus accepts this and even enters into the relationship of "love" for it. This is not because a man wants to be rid of evil things, but because he desires to attain greater freedom and love. And now Jesus says: "Go sell what thou hast and give to the poor." Jesus does not by any means demand that everybody should be poor. Many are to be: those, that is, who "are able to take it". Among men, such people are to be witnesses to the possibility of becoming free from all things; and

as such they are to be a help to those who retain possessions, enabling them to maintain freedom while
using them.

5. JESUS AND MEN

What was the attitude of Jesus towards men and
women?

The New Testament shows him in various relationships: as a child to his parents; as an adult to his
widowed mother; as a kinsman to his relations. He was
the one awaited by his precursor, and the Master to his
disciples. The band of Twelve are marked off from the
other disciples and live on terms of special intimacy with
him. Within the Twelve, the three who were present at
the raising of Jairus' daughter, the Transfiguration, and
in Gethsemane, are even closer to him than the rest.
These are Peter, James and John. The last of these is
"the disciple whom Jesus loved" (John 13. 23; 21. 7).

He was bound by a special tie of friendship to the
family at Bethany, and within that family he was particularly attracted to Mary (Luke 10. 38 ff.). He had another equally close attachment with Mary of Magdalen,
who is found beside his grave at Easter (John 20. 11 ff.).

Then there is the crowd: the people with their
needs, their longing for salvation, unreliable and
changeable. A whole series of individuals can be singled
out from among them: those whom he had helped, such
as the deaf-mute, the cripple, the blind man, the grate-
ful leper, the centurion and his servant, and the woman
with an issue of blood.

And there were many enemies, among whom, again,
were such individuals as the inhospitable Pharisee.
There were people who wanted to embarrass or hinder

him, the disciple who betrayed him, and the individuals who took part in the events of his last two days.

That is to say, there were human relationships of all kinds, which gave scope to all kinds of different feelings of sympathy, attachment, animosity and strife. Can we find some characteristic attitude of Jesus in all this?

He approached men with an open heart. He was almost always to be found in the company of people. He had no house of his own where he could be alone: he was a guest wherever he lived. We might almost say that he had no "private life" at all. He was sensitive to men's needs and full of an inexhaustible readiness to help them. We recall words like these: "Come to me, all you that labour and are burdened; and I will refresh you" (Mat. 11. 28), or: "And seeing the multitudes, he had compassion on them; because they were distressed and scattered abroad like sheep that have no shepherd" (Mat. 9. 36); or the parable of the shepherd who had lost one animal from his flock.

On the other hand, he was reserved towards men, even towards his closest friends. He always remained peculiarly detached. John says: "Jesus would not give them his confidence; he had knowledge of them all, and did not need assurances about any man, because he could read men's hearts" (John 2. 24–5). He wanted nothing from men. Between him and men there was no community of mutual interests, not even one of common work. We never find him portrayed attempting to clarify an issue in common with his companions, or seeking with them a way to become master of some situation. We do not even find him working together with them. Apart from occasions devoted to common worship, like the Paschal meal, he is never even seen pray-

ing with them. And the only time he did look for com-
fort of human companionship, he did not find it:
"Could you not watch one hour with me?" (Mat. 26.
40).

And so a continual solitude enveloped Jesus. There
were always men about him, but among them he was
alone.

His solitude arises because no one understands him.
His enemies do not understand, the multitude does not,
but neither do his disciples. The depth of this lack of
understanding is revealed by a series of incidents. For
example, there is the shattering experience described in
Mark 8. 14 ff. They are together in a boat on the lake.
He had been speaking about the leaven of the Pharisees
and they assume that he is talking about the provisions
they had forgotten to bring with them. So he says
plainly: "Why do you discuss the fact that you have no
bread? Do you not yet know or understand? Have you
still your heart blinded? Having eyes, see you not? And
having ears, hear you not?" Then he reminds them of
the recent miracle of feeding the multitude. "How do
you yet not understand?" Or, we can recall the scenes
when he was arrested and put to death; or the sense in
which they understood his message about the coming of
the kingdom of God right up to and including the time
after Easter (Acts 1. 6).

This lack of understanding constitutes to a decisive
degree Jesus' fate. To see how deep that misunderstanding was, we have only to note the radical change which
took place in the attitude of the disciples after Pentecost. Thus, the life of Jesus is lacking in every presup-
position for *being understood.* It is well to be quite
clear in our minds just how much this meant.

We gain the impression of a rigid isolation; a mute-ness in spite of much speaking. For life only begins to unfold before us from the heart of the other; and the word we speak is only perfected in the ear of one who understands. It is this isolation of Jesus which St John tries to express in his Prologue in terms of the barrier which is raised up between him and the world: "And the darkness did not comprehend it (the light) . . . He came unto his own and his own received him not" (John 1. 5, 11). Connected with this is the impression we get of the futility, in the ordinary sense, of the activity of Jesus. With most religious leaders in history, their new message usually began to be felt, after a period of struggle, within their own lifetime. By contrast, Jesus was to see no return at all; we are reminded of the picture of the grain of wheat which must die before it can bring forth fruit (John 12. 24); even in his disciples. This misunderstanding did not arise merely because his message was too lofty, but because it came from a God whom no one knew, and because between his message and mankind there lay the indispensable revolution in values which the Gospel calls *metanoia* (repentance). For this reason understanding could only come through the Holy Spirit who was to be sent by that selfsame God.

It might now be asked why this Spirit had not come sooner, in Jesus' own lifetime; or why he who supported Jesus' being—see the account of the baptism—and accomplished his words, had not been transmitted to his audience. This is a circle which we are unable to break. People do not understand because the Holy Spirit has not come to them. He does not come, because they are not ready for him. Yet this very preparedness is itself a gift of the Holy Spirit. Thus, normal thinking can find a way neither in nor out. This is the mystery of the new beginning in God himself, and as such it is inscrutable.

But this much is certain: Jesus' message fell on deaf ears.

It was his existence, even more than what he said, that remained misunderstood, for it and his message were one. What his message was if we consider it as doctrine and proclaimed potentiality is that he himself was as an existent being. Let us take the concept of the focal point of existence. This is the spiritual fulcrum on which men balance their lives, the point of departure from which they approach both men and things and to which they return from them again. The greater and more exalted the personality, the deeper lies this focal point. Whether or not a man understands other men depends upon his capacity for observation and sympathy, upon his power to see things as a whole, and penetrate them; but most of all it depends upon the extent to which his own depth of existence is equal to or greater than that of others. We will have more to say about the nature of Jesus' existence later; but we may say here that the starting-point from which he looked upon, judged and confronted men, rejoiced and suffered, are obviously unfathomably deeper than that of his environment. For Jesus there was no such thing as a "we" in the sense of a direct community of existence, but only in the sense of a sovereign love which loves before others are capable of loving, and without their being capable of reciprocating the love shown them. Scarcely a single act of genuine communal existence is recorded in the Gospels; scarcely one true "we" in the strict sense of the term. Not even in prayer is it ever expressed. The résumé of his message from the Father, and the basis of the proper relationship to him, were given by Jesus in the prayer, Our Father. The subject of the Our Father is the "we" of the Christian: but Jesus never repeated this prayer with his disciples, never included himself with this "we". There is no place, as far as I can see, where he took the lead in joining together with his disciples in prayer. Where he himself is seen to pray, as for example at the end of the Last Supper, and still more strikingly, in the Garden of Olives, he speaks and adopts an attitude which no other man can imitate.

6. EMOTION IN THE LIFE OF JESUS

Another equally instructive question is that concerning the part played by feeling in the life of Jesus.

In him we observe various kinds of emotional reaction. These show us that he was not cold and aloof, either by nature or by self-discipline. Thus we learn that he had pity on the people because of their suffering (Mat. 9. 36); that he "looked at and loved" a man in whom something special was going on (Mark 10. 21); that he was irritated by the hypocrisy of those who watched to see if he would heal the sick on the Sabbath: he looked "round about on them with anger" (Mark 3. 5); that he expressed anger at the stupidity of the disciples: "Do you not yet know or understand?" (Mark 8. 17); that he "rejoiced in the Holy Spirit" at the return of those whom he had sent out (Luke 10. 21), and so on. Obviously the sick and the suffering would never have come to him with such confidence; children would never have approached him for a blessing had they not felt a warm sympathy emanating from him. And the accounts about Gethsemane and Golgotha indicate anything but an unimpressionable nature or the attitude of one who was a stern ascetic, above all emotion.

And we could cite many other examples. In spite of this, however, the impression we have of Jesus' nature is one of complete calm under all conditions, a calm which has the same origin as his fearlessness.

This is revealed most clearly in connection with his mission. He proclaimed publicly that the kingdom of God was about to come openly and that the transformation of history, awaited by the prophets, was about to come to pass. This depended, however, upon the acceptance of his message by those who were being called. And so, it might be assumed, he must have been experiencing great excitement, wondering whether this would happen. In fact, we find no trace of this at all. His words and acts are not one whit different from what they are at every moment, as dictated by the will of the Father. When the moment of decision urges, Jesus does nothing to alter the course of events or to ease their effects. This attitude is made particularly clear once the decision has been taken. For example, the scene at Caesarea Philippi shows that it does not arise from any lack of feeling (Mat. 16. 21 ff.). When Jesus began to speak of the terrible things which were to happen to him and Peter tried to remonstrate with him, we are told that he turned and upbraided him (Mat. 16. 23). It was as though he could not bear to hear anything that might upset his decision, and one feels how his inner calm was being threatened by the horror of what was to happen. All the more impressive, therefore, is the way in which his calm continues, the way it lasts through all his experiences and enables him to go on teaching and helping men, strengthening him never to allow himself to be deflected by one hairbreadth from the perfect course of his mission, but, moment by moment, to perform all that that mission requires.

Let us stress once more, however, that in all this there is no trace of the imperturbability of the Stoic or the renunciation of a Buddha. Jesus is fully alive, fully sentient, fully human. His deep calm and human warmth in a situation which was becoming increasingly hopeless revealed what John meant when he wrote: "Peace I leave with you; my peace I give unto you; not as the world giveth, do I give unto you. Let not your heart be troubled; nor let it be afraid" (John 14. 27). These words are all the more significant because they were spoken on the last occasion when he was with his friends, just before the end.

7. JESUS' ATTITUDE TOWARDS LIFE AND DEATH

Now we must touch upon another topic which also throws light on the life of Jesus: his attitude towards life in the obvious sense of the word.

In the total economy of human existence it is the spirit that makes it possible to venture forth from the immediate world of things and one's own nature and become creative. However, the growth of the spirit is not without its dangers: it can cause difficulties in one's adaptation to life; be a hindrance to bodily development and also to the unfolding of the emotional life. Genius can lead either to the utmost limit of human development or beyond it to a sheer pathological state. Religious genius is no exception. We have, for example, the man with extraordinary religious gifts who dies young. In such cases we refer to an early maturity or say that he had an unearthly quality about him. Or there is the man who seems to be a borderline case, the visionary who enjoys very poor health, the mystic with a dangerous penchant for suffering, the man threatened by demons, and so forth.

What is to be said about Jesus in this connection?

Is he a man in whom the spirit loomed so large that his very constitution was devoured by it so that he died, as it were, from inside? Not at all. Jesus gives an impression of perfect vigour. When he died he had, humanly speaking, immeasurable possibilities left which could have been realized had there been time and opportunity.

His personality and life are in no respect those of one who attains perfection and then dies in the flower of youth; his life was destroyed from outside, by violence. Jesus constantly gave the impression that he was infinitely more as a being than was apparent on the surface; that he could do more than he did, that he knew more than he revealed. His death showed that he possessed incalculable reserves of strength and life.

What of the second type? Is Jesus one of those religious persons who are borderline cases and, for that very reason, are able to comprehend and perform the special tasks entrusted to them?

He is not this type either. In him we find no trace of that biological and psychic instability we encounter so often in religious psychology and pathology; nor of that oscillation in emotional states between an extraordinary and unhuman exhilaration and a weakness and depression far below the normal. The only scene that might suggest such a state is Gethsemane, but this has a totally different meaning.

Nor can we induce this kind of psychic structure from his eschatological consciousness, holding, for instance, that he first lived in expectation of a colossal upheaval in the power of the Spirit, but that when this failed to materialize he went to the other extreme and fixed his hopes upon a dialectic of annihilation, hoping to gain through destruction what had not been attainable the other way. Such an explanation would make sense only if we could suppose a nature it would suit: and there is no trace of this at all. The eschatological awareness of Jesus was of a totally different kind, not to be explained in terms of the presuppositions of religious psychology.

The essential character of Jesus shows no hint of melancholy, that commonest of all pathological religious symptoms. He never knew a moment's real depression. His repeated retreat into solitude was not the escape of the melancholic from man and from the light of day: it was the result of a longing for peace in the presence of God, especially at times of momentous decision; and even more than this, it was the entry into that exclusive relationship in which he knew he stood to him whom he called his Father.

Jesus was no visionary either, visited by apparitions of the supernatural or the future, oppressing him at least as much as they exalt him. Nor was he an apocalyptic so acutely conscious of God's threatening wrath that everything around him, even his own life, seemed in imminent danger of collapsing.

He gave the impression of perfect health. We never hear of his being ill or having to be nursed, or of his being weakly or overworked and needing a respite. He led the arduous life of an itinerant preacher, and there is no hint that he ever had to exert every ounce of his strength in order to carry on. The account which tells how he was too weak to carry the beam of the cross to the place of execution (Mat. 27. 32), taken in conjunction with what he had just gone through and with what was taking place within him, does not contradict this fact. On the contrary, we cannot comprehend how he was able to bear so much. The same is true of his rapid death (John 19. 33). As a rule it was a long time before a crucified person died; but we do well to remember that death comes not only from the body, but also from the spirit.

We have still to deal with the question of Jesus' relationship to death. What is said here presupposes, of course, that the Gospels do not indulge in fantasies. That they should have done so seems absurd, for they would have had to choose either to portray a mythical figure, in which case the unreality of the figure would have been immediately apparent, for mythical figures have no psychology and are mere idealizations, whereas Jesus is full of the most concrete life—or to invent a pattern of life quite unknown to men, in which case improbabilities would occur at every turn.

If, then, we accept the Gospel narrative as true, we must admit that the thought of death was not present in the mind of Jesus in the way in which it is in our minds. Each time he spoke of his dying—he did this five times —he connected this with his resurrection.

For us, death is simply the end. Our immediate awareness of life does not penetrate beyond that. True, we say that the essential thing about our life cannot come to an end with death. We express this in various presentiments, metaphors and hopes; and the hope of eternal life is assured by faith in revelation. With Jesus, however, the matter was quite different. He knew that he was to die and accepted death : but he viewed it as a passage to an existence involving both soul and body which would immediately follow after death: "From that time Jesus began to show his disciples that he must go to Jerusalem and suffer many things from the elders and scribes and chief priests; and be put to death, and the third day rise again" (Mat. 16. 21). These are no casual words: they proceed from a general attitude, from an original and unique mode of being in life.

To regard such sayings as retrospective explanations in the light of the later Paschal experience of the disciples would be to distort everything.

For Jesus, the concept of death and resurrection which they express is fundamental to his whole person. As soon as this idea is removed from the picture it is not a real man who is left, much less the truer one one might have thought would emerge when stripped of his mythological trappings—his whole nature and reality vanish. The span of life of which he was directly aware did not end for him, as it does for us, at the approach of death, thereafter to be resumed again tentatively; it passed with perfect clarity right through death. For him, death was not the end but a point of transition; and not at all—to make the point quite clear—in the sense that nothing led beyond death but hope. The way in which Jesus felt himself to be alive, spiritually and bodily, was of such a kind that it reached far beyond death. It saw this as an event within life itself. This total view of life has, of course, nothing in common with any mythology or esoteric certitude: it derived from the reality of God, the beginning and end of all his existence.

The Christian conception of life, death and resurrection is based on Jesus' knowledge of life. It is something more than an assurance of spiritual indestructibility. It is the hope of an eternal human existence in God himself. But the reality in and with whose accomplishment it is found to be possible is Jesus' sense of life. Here

again the decisive thing is not what he says but what
he is.

All this leads us to the conclusion that he lived and
died in a different way from us. And this reveals, in all
its greatness and clarity, what we have already met before when talking of his "health"; it is something more
than mere natural vitality or the spiritual will to live.
It is a quality of his psychosomatic existence for which
there is no standard of measure based on our natural
knowledge.

We can perhaps get some hint of what this means
from the power to endure and to suffer, which can
spring from personal love, or from the spirit's pure will
to create; or from a truly religious sense of duty and
will-power. In mere men, however, this "health" has to
assert itself in spite of the disorders and malformations
which are found even in the healthiest of us. But in
Jesus there was nothing like this whatever. He was
utterly sound and alive, but in a special sense. An
animal can be healthy in terms of its own nature. Man
who has turned from God would like to be healthy but
he cannot be. He was created to exist in dependence on
God: this is his health, which he lost once and for all
by sin. That "health", by contrast, which we com-
monly speak about, is altogether a problematic thing.
One is even tempted to say that it is more enigmatic
than sickness; for what is it after all but sickness so en-
trenched as to have become normal? The ontological
sickness of the fallen creature which disguises its own
total disorder under cover of a relative order? There is
nothing like this in Jesus. In him is the fullness of that
which this confusion has upset: existence from God,
directed to God, life in the Pneuma of God. Therefore,

our notion of health, worked out inevitably on the basis of our experience, does not apply to Christ. His state is altogether beyond our notions of sickness and health.

It is St John again who analyses and puts plainly into words what appears in the Synoptics as a simple, and hence elusive, reality. In St John's Gospel our Lord says to the disciples: "I am . . . the life" (14. 6); and to Martha: "I am the resurrection and the life; he that believeth in me, although he be dead, shall live" (11. 25). This is a theological expression of what the Synoptics present as an objective fact.

"Psychology", however, can do no more than indicate that we are in the presence of something very special, of a state of affairs which is expressed not merely in conceptual propositions, but in a living attitude; in the way, that is, in which personality and life are built up; by means of words which are the double of an existence or form of life to which nothing in any other man corresponds.

Further than this psychology cannot go. It can only point out a direction to follow and show how this human-superhuman reality, once accepted by faith, appropriated in love, and put into practice in deed, makes possible an attitude to life which man could never have achieved by himself. That is to say, psychology can try to exhibit the Christian sense of life and death. If it does this, it will once more reach its limit at the point where the believer's "Christ in me" emerges, the point at which the real *synergeia*, accomplishment in and with Christ, begins.

The nature of Christ cannot be deduced from a study of the psychology of the religious man in general and the Christian in particular. The Christian can exist only in terms of a Christ who eludes psychological analysis as long as this is honestly pursued. If it is not honestly pursued, however—and as a general rule it is not—then it makes no sense at all and becomes merely another tool in the hands of self-glorifying man who uses it to prove that there never was a God-man.

III

THE PROBLEM OF THE
STRUCTURE OF PERSONALITY

1. GENERAL REMARKS

In order to understand a man intellectually we must know what the structures or patterns of his personality are. By "structures" we mean the various types according to which it is possible for a man to be a man, those patterns of human existence that embrace more than any single individual and less than the concept of human nature as such: for example, the "melancholic temperament", the "youth", the "artist", and so forth.

It is worth noting, however, that, in fact, there are no such things as pure structural patterns, but only compounds in which, while one aspect tends to predominate, all the rest are present in one way or another. No artist is merely an artist: he is always influenced by some theoretical or economic factors as well, but the latter are subordinate to the former and to a certain extent conditioned by it.

In any concrete personality we will always find different structures according as we view it from different angles. Thus we might say about a certain man that he was an artist in terms of talent; melancholic by temperament; inclined to be a mystic in religion; an idealist or activist with respect to the hard facts of everyday life; gregarious or a lone wolf, a revolutionary or a sound citizen, socially; normal or manic-depressive medically speaking; and so forth.

Then there are differences with respect to historical period, race, religion or age. If we take all these things into account, the structure of a concrete personality becomes a highly complex thing, always specified, however, by certain dominant features.

Strictly speaking, any intelligible association of forms may be termed a "structure". Every element in such a structure is always related to the other elements: each element is determined by those around it and it in turn reacts upon its surroundings. In other words, the single element is related to the whole, and the total context in turn is related to the single element. It is not difficult to understand, therefore, what we mean when we say that a particular individual has such-and-such a make-up or personality. Understanding the term in this sense, it is not difficult to reply to the question whether the personality of Jesus has such a structure. The obvious answer is that it has. This amounts to no more than saying that his nature is not chaotic.

Here, however, we are concerned with the special meaning of the word, i.e. with those typical figures of human existence which are the key to our understanding of the phenomenon of man as such.

2. THE STRUCTURES OF GROWTH

We shall begin with those structures which have a bearing on the growth of a personality. Can we discover in Jesus any typical form of character evolution, of psychological development?

The idea of "evolution" is a widely accepted notion today, but we do well to remind ourselves that it is only recently that this has become so. In general it is connected with the new awareness of history which began with the Renaissance and became dominant in the nineteenth century. According to this concept, life, when it begins, is a very simple form, full, however, of potential variations, not just any variations, but those that are determined by the natural law governing the living thing in question. These potentialities unfold, according to the conventional picture, in the sense that the inherent forms emerge and become differentiated and the thing becomes more specifically distinct and more complex until maturity is reached; then it stops, and gradually decline sets in. Progress from the state of potentiality to manifest fullness is felt to be something natural and even beautiful, a real disclosure of creative energy. The Middle Ages thought otherwise. The men of those days held that a perfect existence would have to be endowed with the fullness of developed life, with consciousness and maturity, from the beginning. We feel today that this way of looking at things is contrary to nature. We accept as axiomatic that self-development and self-fulfilment are part of the essence of life.[1]

However, crises occur along the path of development. Its course is not always or necessarily a smooth one: it may proceed by characteristic stages like the ages of man, for instance. These stages of development begin,

[1] "Development" means self-emergence from a generative milieu. But it is possible to conceive of another type of growth according to which the living thing is only partly determined by what is inside it. For the rest it reacts against stimuli received from its environment and by so doing forms itself into something new. Thus a living principle could absorb from without or produce from within something entirely new, and do so to a limit that is *a priori* indeterminable. But we cannot pursue this thought here.

unfold and reach their final stability while the next phase is already beginning to take shape beneath them. So they struggle together, disturb and interfere with one another until finally the new phase asserts itself. But we can also have aberrant developments, hypertrophies or fixations, deviations which have to be overcome—sometimes with great difficulty. Otherwise they may harden and establish themselves permanently.

What kind of growth do we encounter in the life of Jesus? More basically, is there any "evolution" to be observed in him at all?

The question is not an easy one to answer because the span of his life covered by the biblical texts is so very brief and the information so meagre. A few bare facts can be gleaned from Luke about his infancy and boyhood; about his youth and early manhood there is nothing at all. We have details only for the period of his public ministry, which was of short duration. Moreover, the evangelists are not interested in biographical details. They are not writing a "Life of Jesus", but recounting events, acts and situations which have a bearing on the message of salvation. Thus, innumerable facts and circumstances which would have been interesting to us from the standpoint of the spiritual biography of Jesus are passed over in silence.

The accounts about his birth and early life lay very great stress on the fact that the child's character was far different from that of ordinary men. The true nature of his extraordinariness is seen, however, if we compare these authentic reports with those to be found in the apocryphal Gospels or other, later, legends. The latter depict Christ as an already mature and superior being who is childlike only externally, but otherwise stands quite apart from the rest of mankind.

By contrast, the extraordinariness revealed by the biblical accounts is of quite a different kind. The child is presented as fully human in every respect, a *perfectly normal individual,* even to the extent of having his life endangered by the ferocity of an angry king and of being subject to the authority of his parents. Yet, right in this normality and utterly without anything the least bit miraculous, there shines a depth—or a height—of consciousness which, like some new sensory centre not definable in terms of normality, brings normality itself into a new perspective.

St Luke's account of the pilgrimage to Jerusalem when Jesus was twelve years old (2. 41 ff.) continues the story of the circumcision and the presentation in the Temple (2. 21 ff.). Just as he had fulfilled the Law in the former instance by means of his parents, so he now fulfils it in person by making the customary Passover pilgrimage to Jerusalem for the first time at the age of twelve. The account also continues what we have been told about his conception and birth in 2. 1 ff.: that he indeed had a human mother, but that his father was God himself. The incarnation thus goes back to a special creative act on the part of God, to the intervention of the Holy Spirit. We are, then, told that the boy was already aware that he belonged immediately to God. Until this time he will presumably have lived like any other child, and as far as the following years are concerned, we learn at the end of the account that "he went down with them and came to Nazareth and was subject to them". Nevertheless, in the depths of his spirit he is detached from his earthly environment and from parental authority. His true home is not Nazareth but the house of his Father in heaven, the Temple; and the true guide of his life is not his earthly parents but the will of his Father, compared with which even the greatest care of his nearest and dearest must take second place.

There is nothing miraculous about the scene itself. The annals of religious biography can show examples of vivid spiritual awareness and a definite feeling of belonging to God at ages much below Jesus' twelve years. What is unique is the content of Jesus' awareness. Comparing it with that which he later had as an adult, we see that there was no qualitative difference between the child's relation to the Father and that of the adult to the Father; while his remark about his Father as a twelve-year-old differs from the way any other twelve-year-old would speak about the heavenly Father, in the same way that the Father-relationship of the Master differs from the belief in Providence of any adult believer.

This has a double significance for our inquiry. It shows that we cannot say anything about the time when, or the way in which, this awareness began. The recorded experience itself cannot be explained as an irruption into his consciousness of his belonging to the Father; as though the child, who had lived hitherto in the manner of any other pious child of his age and environment, now suddenly discovers his relationship to God, being impressed and moved by the Temple and its worship, by the sight of the capital and its history, by the piety of his parents and the great crowds of people; as though he should become aware of himself as God's child and at the same moment become what he knows himself to be. There is not the slightest hint that this is what took place. There is no indication that there was any irruption of a new awareness; on the contrary, the account demonstrates the existence of a relationship which has its source in the certainty of an already existing awareness. The decisive factor in the personality of Jesus was already there. On the other hand, we must see this relationship as one completely consistent with a person of his tender years, for verse 52 states, explicitly, that he advanced from then on to youth and manhood.

The awareness of his relationship to the heavenly Father; the fact that in the centre of his being he had become a stranger to all the relationships of family and environment; his immediate reference to the Father, running like a constant through everything—all this is perfected within the framework of a psychology appropriate to boyhood, but is not reducible to the terms of such a psychology.

There already exists, in other words, a sense of belonging to and of being guided by the heavenly Father, which contains within itself the whole essence of what will come later on. But this awareness is thoroughly imbedded in the pattern of experience appropriate to his stage in life, so that there is continuous growth. It is, in fact, a growth "in wisdom, age, and grace", not merely before men, but also "before God", as the text informs us.

Neither here nor later is there any break-through into ultimate reality.

Such things only occur if one imposes a preconceived pattern of religious evolution on the events in the life of Jesus, and interprets them accordingly.

It is typical for a great religious personality to undergo a revolution in his relationship to the world and to himself, what is called "conversion" in the psychology of religion. Before this occurs, the individual in question was caught up in the stream of life and behaved like anyone else, perhaps he even manifested a more passionate devotion to the world than others; then suddenly, a spiritual change takes place, which may have been caused by various things: a chance meeting with some impressive religious personality, meditation on the vanity of all earthly things, the impact of some terrible event. This helps him to become aware of the true meaning of life as compared with the illusions of the world; gives him a sense of what is ultimately important and urgent so that all else seems trivial and superfluous; shows him what his life ought to have been and so makes him realize how fruitless, wicked and even disastrous his previous life has been. The holiness of God lays bare the desolate state of man. His encounter with destruction and new creation causes him to regard himself as another person, the true man at last, who has been endowed with a new principle of life and a new type of existence.

Some have tried to interpret in this light the baptism of Jesus in the Jordan which reaches a climax in the sentence: "This is my beloved Son, in whom I am well pleased" (Mat. 3. 13 ff.; Mark 1. 9 ff.; Luke 3. 21 ff.). In point of fact, however, there is no evidence that anything was making its appearance now which was not present before. The statement concerns, not an "experience", a psychological reaction, but a reality. It is not Jesus who "experiences": it is the Father who *declares*. He declares not what Jesus now becomes, but what he already is. "The Spirit" does not transform a devout man into the Messiah, by descending upon him: he fills with his whole power him who is by nature the Messiah, at the moment when he grants the Old Dispensation its last due and inaugurates the New. Again, it does

not mean that Jesus had previously been a stranger to
the Father and to the Spirit. Had that been the case,
John, who was "filled with the Holy Ghost from his
mother's womb" (Luke 1. 15) would have been greater
than he whom he preceded. What we really have here is
a description of a divine coming and in-pouring, for the
psychology of religion has no standards of comparison,
for the very good reason that in this way for the first
time is revealed he who until then had been the unknown God. We can find out what a real experience of
break-through is like by comparing the biblical text to
other accounts, for example, those describing the experiences of Buddha or Mohammed.

If the texts are allowed to speak for themselves and
are not altered in form or meaning or general feel by
having a preconceived pattern imposed on them, we are
obliged to admit that there is no evidence in the New
Testament that Jesus ever became what he had not yet
been in his essential relationship to God his Father. On
the contrary, his character, attitude and behaviour make
it clear that he was at the beginning the same person
that he was at the end. We can speak of an "evolution"
of his personality only in a sense that does not contradict
this fact; more precisely, in a sense that presupposes it.
That is to say, such an evolution must be thought of as
growth within a pattern which from the very beginning
is fully significant. The assertion that such a process is
a psychological impossibility is not only no objection to
the fact that we have to do here with an existence of a
very special kind, but proves this very fact.

The question whether Jesus was subject to any kind
of evolutionary process at all and how, brings us to a
further matter. We have already seen that development

does not necessarily proceed at a smooth pace; it may go by fits and starts; the pattern of one phase may come into conflict with that of a previous phase and be obliged to assert itself, against opposition; crises of different kinds may develop in this way, perhaps particularly so in the case of the religious man, because he is subject to acute tensions and must make a great effort to discipline himself. It is legitimate to inquire, therefore, how Jesus fared with regard to this kind of development.

There are three events in his life which have to be considered here: his temptation and sojourn in the desert after his baptism, his transfiguration while on the final journey to Jerusalem, and the hour he spent in the Garden of Gethsemane, whose full meaning was only revealed in the experience of abandonment on the cross.

The story of his temptation (Mat. 4. 1 ff.; Mark 1. 12 ff.; Luke 4. 1 ff.) might be explained as a typical first crisis in the life of one who was conscious of having a religious mission, somewhat as follows: First of all, in times of stress and spiritual crisis, tensions are increased, powers are at their maximum and spiritual content is matured. A new and more perfect personality is born at such times. The question then has to be debated: Shall this personality subordinate itself to the mission it has received, or shall it dare all alone, confident in its extraordinary powers? The temptation in the Gospels is heightened by the fact that it is conjoined with the experiences of elevation and power and with the feeling of a growing attenuation of surrounding reality which are readily induced by a prolonged fast. The crisis is finally and successfully overcome, the attack thwarted by a mighty exertion of Jesus' will.

If we examine the biblical texts of the temptation

more closely, however, we see that they have a totally different meaning. There is no trace in them at all of "temptation" in the ordinary sense of the word: of an upsurge of desire, a revolt against law, a confusion of values. Nor does the person who is attacked appear to be under any strain. If "temptation" means that the enticement causes an echoing response in the soul of the person being tempted, because of some secret inclination to revolt lurking there, then we have no trace of temptation here. And if "victory" means that there must be some inner struggle, then there was no victory either. The attack simply glanced off. The purpose of the incident is not to show how Jesus vanquished an attack of Satan, but to show how completely he is removed from the sphere where temptation operates and how powerless Satan is against him. This is exactly what he declared later, when he said: "For the prince of this world cometh; and in me hath not any thing. But [he will try his will] that the world may know that I love the Father, and as the Father hath given me commandment, so do I" (John 14. 30–1). The events just described do not relate to any real temptation at all: the incident is a revelation of the absolute unity of the will of Jesus with that of God.

Such unassailability might, indeed, create the impression that Jesus was a lifeless and unreal being. But the opposite is the case. This person so divinely sure of himself is very much alive, very human—but once more we are beyond the limits of psychology, strictly speaking.

His transfiguration on the mountain (Mat. 17. 1 ff.; Mark 9. 1–7 [2–8]; Luke 9. 28–36) and the prayer in the Garden of Gethsemane (Mat. 26. 30 ff.; Mark 14. 32 ff.; Luke 22. 39 ff.) are closely related events. Both took place after a decision had been made: the first on the way to Jerusalem, the second in Jerusalem itself. One is tempted to interpret these events, psychologically, in the light of the man with a mission, as instances of a great upsurge of mental and bodily powers which was then followed by utter depression. The explanation might run somewhat as follows:

He was transfigured "on a high mountain", representing the unity of inner experience and external environment. His whole figure and clothing were radiant —this is symbolical of the highest potential of mental and physical powers. Two prominent Old Testament figures, Moses and Elias, appear and talk with him about his death—an indication that he had the approval of the Old Covenant and that his impending death was sanctioned in heaven. Finally, the Father's voice itself is heard, declaring, shortly before his death, what he had declared reassuringly at the time of his baptism and commanding the disciples to heed his words. It has been decided that he is to die, so he goes to Jerusalem where the end is to come, filled with a willingness to sacrifice himself and a firm confidence in his resurrection (Mat. 16. 21; 17. 22–3; 20. 17 ff.). In spite of, or perhaps because of, the absence of any possible alternative, his sense of special mission is at its climax.

Then comes the collapse, hastened by the shock and exhaustion of the hopeless struggle during the last days in Jerusalem. After he had given his disciples the utmost of his wisdom and love at the Last Supper—had actually given them himself when he instituted the "new covenant in his blood"—he went out into the darkness of night and, alone among his disciples, there occurred the inevitable reaction. He fell into an agony of despair to the extent of revealing pathological symptoms, as the statement about the sweat of blood shows.

He begged for mercy and then pulled himself together and once more felt the reassuring union with the will of God. In some such way as this would psychology interpret the events. But an explanation of this kind would destroy the whole meaning of the events recorded in the Gospels.

This becomes clear if we compare these accounts with others in the Bible which do deal with periods of crisis in the course of a religious mission. The best example is that of Elias, described in the Third Book of Kings. There we read of the tremendous tension accompanying the judgement of God, the subsequent sentence imposed on the priests of Baal, the miraculous appearance of the rain, and his running before the king's chariot in ecstasy; then we learn of the prophet's collapse in the wilderness, his strengthening by an angel, and the great revelation made to him on Mt Horeb (chaps. 18–19). One thing is clear: the actions described exceed the capacity of the man who performs them. In the performance of the actions he rises far above himself, only to sink down afterwards lower than any normal man. It is not the prophet who does these things, but a power that takes hold of him, and then leaves him limp when it departs. This is perfectly obvious in the case of Elias; but it is also more or less true in all other experiences of this kind. With Jesus, on the one hand, the situation is completely different. He always remains himself whatever he does or suffers. Whatever he does is never beyond his ability to do it, but appears as the logical outcome of that ability. His experiences on the mountain and in the garden, for example, were not, in themselves, abnormal; they were the revelation on a grand scale of what was ever present in him: the meaning and power of himself and his mission, and also the awfulness of the sacrifice which the Father was demanding of him.

Another thing needs to be stressed here, too. The existence of the prophet—and that of the apostle too (cf. 1 Cor. 4. 9 ff.)—contains *a priori* the necessary inadequation between mission and being, between office and ability. Mission and office are imposed on him, and to make him capable of fulfilling his task, strength is given him. In his case there is an alien element intervening which has to be accepted and assimilated, and the psychological process consists in the reconciliation of this dichotomy. But with Jesus things were quite different. Mission and being, task and will, office and ability, were all one. He is what he signifies; he desires that for which he has been sent; he is able to do what he has to do. And so the basis for any mighty upsurge and let-down is absent, as well as for any appropriation of what is not due or any desire to rebel against the given task. He is always himself. There is no split discernible in his character. Indeed, we always get the impression from his behaviour that Jesus possessed great untapped reserves of strength, that he was actually much more than he appeared to be on the surface, and that he was capable of doing much more than he actually did.

Obviously, there was no "crisis" in his case, but the expression of a tremendous experience. Yet this experience was in conformity with his being and, therefore, "natural", revealing itself in the deep calm, self-possession and control which he possessed at all times, in spite of the terrible things that he had to endure.

In Matthew's account of the death of Jesus we encounter the sentence: "And about the ninth hour, Jesus cried with a loud voice, saying: Eli, Eli, lama sabachthani, that is, My God, my God, why hast thou forsaken me?" (27. 46). Mark has almost the identical words (15. 34). At first glance, we might be inclined to interpret this cry as an expression of utter despair, as a sign of the collapse of his entire ego at its very core, his relationship with his Father. The "loud cry" which came later would only serve to enhance this view.

But against this interpretation, we must point out that Luke's version of the death scene does not contain any sentence referring to his abandonment, although the overall picture of the passion and death is the same as in Matthew and Mark. Hence Luke cannot have intended to convey a different impression from the others. Where the other two mention his "crying with a loud voice", Luke has the sentence: "Father, into thy hands I commend my spirit" (33. 46). And thus the "abandonment" in no sense disturbs the mood of deepest trust but unites with it to form a whole attitude. And this attitude obviously conforms to the pattern of the bursts of prayer in the Garden of Gethsemane, in which anguish and pleas for mercy were combined with a perfect submission to the will of the Father; for the death of Christ on the cross cannot be dissociated from the scene in Gethsemane but must be seen as its logical conclusion or consummation. The important decision was made in the garden, it was merely implemented on Golgotha

The significance of Christ's death and his attitude when dying must be understood in the light of his attitude towards life and death in general. This is disclosed by his remarks on his forthcoming passion, in which death and resurrection are seen to be bound up together in an indissoluble whole which it is beyond the grasp of men to penetrate. He who said that he was

destined to die and on the third day rise again (Mat. 16.
21), and repeated this frequently, thus indicating that
it was a matter of great importance, was not one to give
way to despair.

The cry on the cross is no more an expression of
despair than his behaviour in Gethsemane was a sign of
depression. A real feeling of despair at the moment of
death would have shown itself in some other way, and a
genuine collapse of this kind, at the critical moment,
would certainly have begun to manifest itself earlier.

The cry on the cross cannot be explained in terms of
the psychology of religion; it points to the serious
reality of an existence that is beyond our comprehension. We must look into this matter more closely.

3. TEMPERAMENT AND BEHAVIOUR STRUCTURES

In addition to structures of growth, there are also
the others, those that determine form of personality,
many-sidedness of temperament and originality of behaviour.

Let us begin with those which pertain to sex.

Jesus was emphatically a man. The fact must not be
allowed to become obscured either by certain conventional ways of portraying him in art or by the types of
piety or devotion which give rise to this portraiture.
Jesus is made to appear as a tender, passive, half-
feminine individual, but this is due to a fatal misinter-
pretation which empties the notions of Jesus' "gentle-
ness", "humility", or "self-sacrifice" of all meaning. It
would be equally erroneous, it must be admitted, to
conceive of his masculinity exclusively in terms of the
man of action, the aggressive type, or the man who is
concerned with superficial notions about honour.

Jesus' manhood was strong, deep-seated, and inspir-ing; but, typically, it was not governed by any passion or impulse: it was ruled entirely by the spirit. This is revealed most clearly in the very centre of his existence, by the way in which he fulfilled his primary task, his mission. He had been charged to proclaim the kingdom of God, to announce its claims to the world and to see that those claims were made effective, if necessary, against the will of the world, yet, in the logic of the redemption, for and on behalf of the world. His task was to take hold of reality and raise it to the realm of grace. He accomplished this mission with such ob-jectivity and subordination of his own will to the task— a subordination which, nonetheless, did not suppress or trammel but liberate his personal will—that he suc-ceeded in realizing thereby the fullest essence of true manhood. The same thing is shown by the calm fear-lessness, arising out of his dedication to his mission, with which he carried out his task to the very end. He neither recoiled from it, evaded it, nor threw himself into it arrogantly; neither yielded nor overreached himself. Again, there was his utter kindness yet fairness; his respect for human freedom; the play he accorded to existence; his way—which only slowly became apparent —of saying, not everything, but the right thing cal-culated to set life in motion, and so on.

On the other hand, an unbiased examination of the evidence shows clearly that his manhood was without trace of any of the baser passions. This is not because the evangelists were at pains to cover up such failings; nor is it because he had no feelings at all like other individuals, or because he was an ascetic and overcame them. A primordial warmth and fullness of life per-vaded his whole personality. But his masculinity was completely integrated in his whole religious personality, more precisely, in a centre which lay deeper and was mightier than the spiritual or religious centre to be found in man. His manhood had been taken over by the divine power of love, understood in the purest sense of the word, and permeated by it. The manhood of Jesus was transformed into perfect, selfless, divine love.

The same sort of thing can be said about his ethnic structure.

The way in which men respond to Christ, the way, indeed, in which his contemporaries felt about him, is curiously contradictory. He was taken to be the son of David, and in the course of the events of which he was the centre, claimed for himself the promises that had been made to David. He was a product of the Old Testament, and its concepts and atmosphere are presupposed by all his sayings. On the other hand, he overstepped the bounds of this world in a very decided way; but not by adopting a cosmopolitan or completely unattached, purely spiritual attitude. There was nothing in common between him and the Sadducees or Herodians. He firmly upheld the Law and held scrupulously to the place which his Father had assigned him in history. This even set certain limitations to his own inclinations. Hence it is just as wrong to view him merely as a figure typical of the Jewish way of life as it is wrong to separate him from it drastically. His descent was more by way of the spirit than by blood; and again, the kinship was more religious than cultural.

We can understand his position only if we realize the deep cleavage in Old Testament history. The significance of this was both great and fateful. The life of the Jewish people ought never to have been the expression of a merely natural national temperament; it should have been a continuously manifested act of faith in divine guidance. The Jewish people's historical existence ought to have let itself be modelled from within by the Spirit. In fact, however, it was a continual rebelling against this destiny, and a thwarting of the realization of its own potentiality as shown it by God. In Jesus, God's plan was perfectly realized, bringing about the final, complete laying bare of the state in which the people of the Covenant found itself. Jesus' genealogy is that of the "spiritual Israel". He belonged to the lineage of promise and faith and prophecy, and had nothing to do with the lineage of self-assertive national consciousness. What the Jewish people should always have done, but actually did so seldom, i.e. ascend by faith above immediate, tangible nature to the realm of the mind and spirit so as to become what God desired them to be, had finally been accomplished in Christ. In him the natural people of Israel—St Paul's "Israel according to the flesh"—had finally been overcome. And so, we understand that those who would not co-operate with him in achieving this purpose saw him as a betrayer of the people and their hopes, whereas those who were prepared to co-operate recognized him without difficulty as one of their own.

However, there is in Jesus something more which lies deeper than "spirit" and "faith". A situation has now been created which cannot be understood in terms of Jewish or non-Jewish, racial or universalist categories. I refer to the element which makes it possible for every man to see him as the Redeemer. Every man can understand Christ by what he knows of himself, without having to identify him ethnically with his own people or, on the other hand, to deny his people for Christ's sake.

Our relationship to him is founded on this fact. It is, therefore, at once completely distorted and upset if we insist on trying to see Jesus in a purely national light, or speak of a Jewish, European, African, ancient or modern Christ.

4. JESUS IS UNIQUE

There are other structures that condition the spiritual life.

We have the philosophically inclined man, the practical man, the artistically creative man, the man of action, etc. But these categories do not seem to be applicable to Jesus. It is not that his nature proves them wrong; they simply do not fit.

It would seem more appropriate to speak of the human type that is immediately interested in man as such, and in the course and ordering of his affairs. Subdivisions of this type give us the helper, the educator, the reformer. But these categories do not really fit either. Things of this kind were not important enough for Jesus to allow us to characterize him in this way. It is true that he loved men, sympathized with their trials, and was anxious to help; but not in the manner of a philanthropist or social reformer. This becomes perfectly clear when we realize that we could say the very opposite; that, basically, Jesus was not concerned to make men happier or improve their earthly lot, but to proclaim the sovereignty of God.

People have seen the "Kingdom of God", which was his greatest concern, in a purely ethical or spiritual sense—or even as something idyllic. It has to do, in reality, with something of absolute religious significance: with God's claim to sovereignty. For his kingdom

Jesus abated not a whit of the demands made by the prophets. Here too, then, we find our habitual structures cut across by something which transcends them.

It would be instructive to ask whether Jesus could be called a "genius".

A man's intelligence can be of many varying degrees, from the purely negative through the average to the extraordinary. Genius means that a particular endowment, a power of knowledge or creativity, action or feeling, is so intense, so productive, so utterly obedient to its inner controls, that it ploughs remorselessly through received convention until it reaches original, primordial truth. Whatever it may produce is marked, not by a quality of mere superiority, but by the authority of essential truth in the strict meaning of the words. In other words, genius is that disposition in man which makes it possible for the fundamental processes of mind, for the basic powers of mankind, for the tendencies of history and of the cosmos, to come fully into their own. Whatever term we may use for it, genius is always the disclosure of some gift, a gift not merited but given; and it presupposes a corresponding disposition for hard work and self-denial. By the same token it can be a risky thing. Mediocrity is safer. Genius is a marginal state, exposed to the dangers of all such states. This may be seen when we consider the relation of the genius to his environment or to himself; for example, in the crises connected with his development, in his tendency to overwork himself, in the frequent maladjustment of the various elements which go to make up his psychosomatic complex, in the appearance of wastage phenomena in domains not immediately connected with his creativity, etc.

The question whether Jesus was a genius was once

considered very important and was instrumental in causing his real significance to be pushed aside as a matter for psychological interpretation. But it is a misleading question. Not even his action on history, let alone his redemptive significance, is an effect of genius. If we use the word in its ordinary sense, we may question whether he was a genius in the psychological or cultural sense at all. He certainly showed no signs of being subject to the crises or turmoil, the phenomenal output or, on the other hand, the wastage associated with the usual image of the genius. Our conclusion, therefore, is that the evidence has been misinterpreted in this regard. But this is not all. We must add at once, so that the deeper truth we are trying to convey may be made plain, that neither as man of ideas nor as man of action, neither in his outward manner and inner reactions nor in his destiny, did Jesus give the impression of being an extraordinary person in the sense in which a genius must be extraordinary if the concept genius is to have any content at all. In Jesus we come face to face with a very special kind of significance. What is it exactly?

We shall perhaps be able to make some progress if we link this question with another. Can Jesus, properly speaking, be classified as belonging to the type known as the religious man? Was he a religious genius?

Religion is the relation with the "other", the "numinous", the mysterious, whatever word we use to describe that which is quite unlike everything else; unlike it and distinguished from it, not merely as truth is distinguished from goodness, or the realm of physics from that of biology, but in a very special sense. Whereas all other things belong to the present sphere, and are, as it were, "on this side", religion belongs to another sphere, to the "other side": the former are "earthly", the latter is "unearthly"; the former natural, immediate, close, penetrable, the latter strange, mysterious, remote, and so on. To have a religious personality is to have a specially acute awareness of these values and realities, to be highly developed both in experience and action with reference to these things, so that the shape of the personality is determined by them. We are dealing, of course, with a disposition like any other disposition. This particular one shows in a given individual the different characteristics and appears in varying degrees of originality and intensity. We must hasten to add at once, that from the point of view of revelation, of our relation to the living God and the business of redemption, this religious disposition has potentialities which can be positive or negative.

Revelation and faith are not at all the same thing as the religious quality of a given person with its concomitant experiences, and they can be endangered by the latter as well as helped by them. In the case of the religious genius the religious disposition achieves that capacity for creative vision and moulding, that closeness to the fundamental reality of things which we mentioned above. That is to say, there are certain inherent dangers present in him which may endanger his own as well as his neighbour's life. The dangers are greater for the religious genius than for other forms of genius because religion has to do with the fundamentals of life.

The personality of Jesus and the course of his life are not marked by any of the crises or danger-signs associated with the religious genius. He does not give the impression of being a man who risks himself in order to disclose some new value. He is sane and self-assured at every point, in control of himself and even of his fate. If we consider his words, actions and destiny, and compare him with persons who were undoubtedly geniuses and *homines religiosi,* we cannot possibly conclude that he is to be classed as a religious genius. Compared with the works of the great mystics or one of the great sermons of Buddha, the Sermon on the Mount appears almost a commonplace thing. The works of the mystics appear to be more profound, more powerful, more moving, more sublime—whatever term you prefer to use to describe that unusualness that is the hallmark of genius—until we realize that a judgement of this kind is not applicable to Jesus.

His true significance is not bound up with what he said, or did, or what happened to him—as one of a type among many others of the same brand—but in what he is. His words and deeds are but sparks emanating from something much deeper, something immeasurably greater than can be described in words. Again, we must not conceive of this being as noteworthy in the usual way, as a mighty, pure, or living personality; as remarkable in a special way that is unlike any other and hard to express in words. In the final analysis, it was not what Jesus did or stood for as a religious figure, but what God accomplished through him that matters; not what he said about God, but the way in which he brought God to us; not that he taught us how to find God, but that God was made present in him. Jesus' place is not on the side whence the act of religion comes; his place is on the side whither it tends as to its object; he must be ranged, not among the pious and devout, but with the end to which the devout address their piety.

This is shown in various ways: in his relation to faith, for example. He is for ever speaking about faith: he asks for it; he arouses it. Faith is not one kind of activity among others: it is the lively response of man to the coming of the kingdom of God. And so, correctly speaking, faith is simply the content of what Jesus calls for, but he himself does not "believe". The word cannot be used with reference to his own existence. He stands, not in the world of men who believe, but in the world to which their belief stretches out. To be more precise: he makes faith possible. Something similar can be said of his relation to his Father. Jesus teaches us to use the Christian "we" when we address the Father. He unites all the faithful in one fellowship, enabling them to say, appropriately, "Our Father". But he himself does not use this "we". He says "I" (Mat. 11. 25; Mark 14. 36; Luke 23. 46; John 11. 41). This "I" does not occupy the same place as the "we" taught us in the Our Father. It is not the singular form of that "we". The "I" which he uses cannot become absorbed in the "we" which he taught men to say: on the contrary, it forms one with the "thou" whom he addresses, in a totally different realm of being. Jesus does not believe, but makes it possible for men to believe. He is not pious, but engenders piety. He does not strive to reach the Creator and Father of all, encouraging men to follow him: he shows us the Father's face and enables us to address him.

Let us return once more to the question being considered. Religious natures can be classified according to certain types. There is the ascetic type in which the religious spirit exhibits itself as a heroic victory over the world. This is often combined with that of the mystic, in whom the vacuum created by this victory over created things is filled up anew and the reality of holiness becomes a matter of immediate experience. There are other types too: the scholar, the wise man, the teacher, etc. There are the reformers, the doctors and educators, the heroes, warriors, conquerors, wonder-workers and poets. Does Jesus fit into any of these types?

In each case there are certain features which may remind us of him. But the moment we examine them more closely, look at the complete picture and compare this with the complete picture of Jesus, we see how completely different he is from any of these types. Especially, anything that might be called religious quest, response, conversion or commitment, is altogether absent from his nature. More important than this, from the very core of his being there streams forth something which you will never find in any of these other religious types and which absorbs his whole "structure". This "something" is the presence in him of "God with us". This *being with us* is not just the universal immanence of God the Creator and Preserver of all things; nor is it the presence of God in the soul of the man who is spiritually alive: he is *with us* in a sense that can be fully and clearly understood only in terms of the Old Testament. The unique quality of what happened in the Old Testament is this: not only did God create all things, not only does he preserve and govern all things, but he declares that he is on his way, coming to mankind. He is the God who is approaching, and his approach draws ever nearer and nearer. Finally, he arrived—in Jesus, plainly, for all men to see. He did not come privately, as a gracious condescension for the benefit of some, or in a spiritual sense only, but in a way that involved a "step" which was fateful for the destiny of God himself, since he had now made the destiny of man his own.

God's coming to be with us in Christ is of a special kind. He lives among men as the "Son of God".

The relationship of man to God is constantly portrayed in religion in terms of the relation between son and father. Strictly speaking, of course, it transcends any relationship whereby one man may be linked to another. But these relationships are so important in human life that they are simply transposed to the religious sphere and serve as patterns for the experience of religious reality. This is proper, too, for our relationship to God is a relationship to him who is Life itself. Hence it follows that in him the essential forms of life do not only become effective; they find in him the plenitude of ultimate meaning. So then, many things about life suggest the appropriateness of this son-father relationship as an image of man's relationship with God: the relationship of begotten to begetter; of younger to older; weaker to stronger; the rising, immature, possessionless, inexperienced, untried generation compared with its established predecessor endowed with power and possessions. The relationship is one based upon authority, love, obedience and confidence. It also, of course, contains the seeds of rivalry on both sides. But this pattern of the relationship which finds expression in the most varied ideas about the fatherly majesty and power of the Divinity, and the reverence and trust in God of man, this pattern which, in certain mythological conceptions about the divinity makes no attempt to conceal the latent conflicts it contains, is quite inadequate even to interpret the Christian's relationship with the revealed Father in heaven, let alone the relationship in which Christ himself stood to him whom he called his Father.

The pattern we have been discussing is based on the

fact that the father gives being to the son and so has both authority over him and responsibility for him: and on the converse fact that the son has received being from the father and therefore has a claim to care from his father and also a duty of reverence towards him. Son and father both grow older; but this does not mean the same thing to each of them. The son becomes stronger, the father weaker. The son grows towards the future, the father retreats into the past. The whole process gives rise to resentment as well as to trust, to mistrust as well as to solicitude, to revolt as well as to reverence. Thus a deep conflict remains latent within the father-son relationship, and this must be settled somehow, either openly or in a veiled manner. The son runs a double risk; he may either maintain his relationship to his father, continuing to live his life as a son—but this will entail the neglect of his own life and his never reaching maturity; or he may develop his own life, become a father himself and in so doing break with his father, usurping his place or abandoning him.

The ultimate psychology of Jesus, or, more exactly, the point where all psychology must admit its inadequacy, is reached when we come to see how this relationship was expressed in his case. His whole existence was founded on his relationship to his Father. It was from him that he had received his mission and the fullness of power (Mat. 12. 27 ff.; John 13. 3); he loved him and was obedient to him (Mark 14. 36; Luke 2. 49; John 5. 30); he regarded as the sum and substance of his whole work the advancement of the kingdom of the Father (Luke 22. 29; Acts 1. 7). No sayings at all can be cited which might suggest that he was seeking a kingdom of his own, that he wanted an independent existence, to make a start for himself, or that he felt cramped by the Father and wished to abandon him or revolt against him. He never departed at any time from the attitude of a son. He preserved this attitude right to the very depths of his personality, it was the very heart of his mission, the very first movement of his most spontaneous feelings. Being a son was his very existence. John expressed this by using the word "remain" and painted the background of this notion in the Prologue to his Gospel, in which he tells how the Son was "with —turned towards—the Father" from all eternity, how he was "in the bosom of the Father". In so being, however, he was in no sense deprived of anything by the Father, kept from maturity, or relegated to a humiliating dependence.

There is no human analogy for this relationship, even in the sphere which is little more than man's great self-portrayal and, at the same time, justification of himself, that of mythology.[1]

Jesus is once and for all and for ever the Son, but a Son who in his Sonship enjoys the perfection of freedom. There is in him no trace of infantilism or rebellion, weakness or resentment, degeneracy or ambition.

We can define his Sonship with reference to its most sensitive point, the point at which conflict seems to lie just beneath the surface: his obedience is equal in dignity to the command which he obeys. He is simply the one who obeys as the Father is the one who commands.

[1] This would be the place to carry out an investigation into the meaning of the various theogony stories: the unmanning of the son gods by the fathers, the overthrow of the father gods by the sons; but this would necessitate too long an excursus on comparative religion.

IV

JESUS' MODE OF EXISTENCE

1. THE PERSON AND EXISTENCE OF JESUS

To the questions already asked we must now add
another concerning his mode of existence. I do not
claim to be able to say anything fundamentally new on
this point; but we may be able to see where the crux of
the matter lies.

Man is not only an *individuum* like a plant or an
animal, but a person. This means not merely that life
appears in a separate, organized form, but that an individual soul together with the body it informs is there
as a single, independent existence.

"Person" does not denote any kind of make-up, e.g.
bodily condition, spiritual power, mental energy, endowment, educational attainment, etc. It is not something which can be expressed in terms of make-up or
psychological content: it is the manner in which all
these things subsist. Person is at once something obvious
and yet logically incomprehensible. It is person that
imparts the essential character to all that goes to make
up a man, not merely by inhering in this or that individual, but by belonging to the "ego" in such a way
that it makes the latter belong to itself. In this way, it
becomes evident not only who the subject of these
attributes, actions and relations is, but further, that an
"I" exists which has a claim upon them and is respon-

sible for them. In what sense, then, can we say that Jesus is a person?

Let us look more closely at those acts in which the factor of independent, personal responsibility is particularly apparent, for example: when Jesus is obeying the Father: when he commands men; when he gives himself to those who believe in him and demands devotion from them in return.

These acts have a special air of perfection about them. This does not spring from the fact that the thing commanded or performed is especially or unusually right, or that it is done in a particularly noble and disinterested manner, but from the way in which it belongs to him who does it.

The quality of the act of command and of the act of obedience, of the giving of self and of the receiving of devotion in return, depends upon the freedom of the performer of the action. He is able to command only to the extent to which he is at one with his own will, which presupposes, of course, that his will is in harmony with the norm of right willing. He is able to obey to the extent to which he can answer for himself. He is able to give himself to others to the extent to which he is in possession of himself. He is able to accept others to the extent to which he is in himself. That is to say, he can perform all these things to the extent to which he is a person and fulfils his personality.

With men this is only partially true. Even the greatest and most perfect of men is not more than approximately himself. He is not fully at one with his own will but is striving to become so. He is not able to answer for himself without reserve, but knows that he should be able to do so, and tries to come to his own support. He does not possess himself, finally and truly, but is searching for himself and struggling to obtain himself. He is not in himself but is on the way to becoming so. All of which points again to the fact that ultimately he is not really truly himself, nor in possession of what belongs to him, but is a freedman who needs the strength and support of the master who has set him free.

For this reason, human freedom is such a problematical thing. A man is free, and yet he is not. It is rather that he is becoming free than that he is already free. That is why, if we consider things properly, we see that his commands are both hesitant and arrogant. Hence too, his obedience takes the form of submission to superior authority, and yet—the inevitable counterpoint—he is ever ready to rebel. That is why he gives himself, yet at the same time cannot really let himself go: he hankers after himself again or becomes a burden to the other. And when the other gives himself, he is unable to accept him and keep him: the other, when he draws near, comes in to somebody who is not at home in his own house. Or else he does accept him but not as a free person; he enslaves him and subjects him.

In this respect, there is in Jesus something radically different from other men; not only in important things, but in little things as well, in mighty deeds as well as in the small gestures, not only in substantive matters but in the whole manner of his behaviour.

In whatever way we view Jesus' relationship to various factors, material objects, possessions, desires, power, work, history, destiny—in all these things it is clear that he succeeds in preserving a manner of being himself which is entirely his own. His is a freedom that is unique. The manner in which he obeys and orders; the manner in which he gives of himself in his acts, his teaching and his mystery, and also receives in return the self-oblation of those who trust him and believe in him, reveals that his activity proceeds from a unique kind of freedom.

Not only is he freer than others, less a slave of inhibitions, more resolute in his decisions, impelled by deeper and stronger motives; there is something here that goes to the root of his being and provides the basis for a new character. This manifests itself, not in any extraordinary performance or behaviour, but in a fundamental tendency, an air of sovereignty which is perceptible in everything and imparts to his whole life and bearing, his speech and his actions, a peculiar existential significance.

It is very difficult to describe what I mean, but this is an attempt:

He gives a special stamp to his obedience to his Father. If we collect all his sayings about the will of the Father and his relation to that will, we see that he identifies his obedience with that will. John 6. 37 ff. may serve as an example of many such sayings: "All that the Father giveth to me shall come to me; and him that cometh to me, I will not cast out. Because I came down from heaven, not to do my own will but the will of him that sent me. Now this is the will of the Father who sent me; that of all that he hath given me, I should lose nothing, but should raise it up again in the last day. And this is the will of my Father that sent me; that everyone who seeth the Son and believeth in him may have life everlasting; and I will raise him up in the last day." Obedience as such is placed on a par with command. It does not arise from the relationship of weaker

to stronger, or of purely factual to normative, but is
itself *qua* obedience, as strong and valid as command.
It is the complying good, as the other is the commanded
good: the two are united in having the same root.

The same attitude dictates his own tone of command
in the Sermon on the Mount: "You have heard that it
was said of them of old . . .", through the Old Testament revelation, that is, through God who is his Father,
"But I say to you." This "It was said to them of old, but
I say to you" expresses the underlying spiritual attitude
of the Sermon on the Mount (Mat. 5. 21, 22, 27, 28, 33,
34, 43, 44). "Heaven and earth shall pass; but my words
shall not pass" (Mat. 24. 35).

Once again it is St John who expressed this thought
in final form. When referring to what his life with Jesus
had enabled him to "see, touch and handle", he put it
this way: "I am the light . . ."; "I am the way, and the
truth and the life . . ." (John 8. 12; 14. 6).

The same underlying assumption leads to the special
manner in which he gives himself, a manner at once
unheard of and convincing: he instituted the mystery
of the Eucharist "for a memorial" of himself. St Luke
says: "And, taking bread, he gave thanks, and brake:
and gave to them, saying: THIS IS MY BODY WHICH IS
GIVEN FOR YOU. Do this for a commemoration of me. In
like manner the chalice also, after he had supped, saying: THIS IS THE CHALICE, THE NEW TESTAMENT IN MY
BLOOD, WHICH SHALL BE SHED FOR YOU" (Luke 22.
19–20). This is still further intensified in the promise
of the mystery as presented by St John: "I am the
living bread, which came down from heaven. If any
man eat of this bread, he shall live for ever: and the
bread that I will give in my flesh, for the life of the

world . . . As the living Father hath sent me, and I live by the Father: so he that eateth me, the same also shall live by me" (John 6. 51–52, 58 [57]). To give his disciples his own Body and Blood as food, and to say that this was being sacrificed for them in atonement for sin, is, humanly speaking, the most appalling nonsense and an example of morbid *hubris*, apart from being disgusting. How could this unheard-of thing hope to be understood and accepted; not only by infatuated disciples who, one might argue, had succumbed to the spell of his overpowering personality and lost the use of their reason, but by men of alert and clear minds and intellectual honesty, drawn from all strata of society and from all degrees of human and spiritual culture, from every time and place?

Precisely because of its enormity, Jesus' giving of himself must be proof against all attack; it must be possible in the nature of things and called for by some inner need of man, otherwise it would surely have failed before the indignation of mankind. Such a gift could only be given because the giver stood free, far removed above the realm of human limitations: free from all that is evil, arid, unnatural and vain, but also, and most important of all, free for himself. He who thus gave himself was not on the way towards finding himself: he was already present, by right, in his own home. He was not seeking himself, he had himself. He had complete and final possession of himself. That is why he could give himself, to be the sacrifice of redemption and the food of new life. Apart from this freedom, every word, every gesture, would have been intolerable.

The uniqueness of this freedom is the expression of the uniqueness of his personality. Jesus was free in a special way quite his own, because he was himself in a special way quite his own.

Being the person one is; being in oneself, living and acting by oneself; going out towards things and then once more withdrawing from them into oneself—in Christ all that was different from what it is in a human existence. The difference is not that it was stronger, greater, calmer, more perfect; it is a qualitative difference. This gives rise to the obviousness and withal strangeness that are so typical of him. From it comes his authority, the like of which is to be found in no other being.

From this derives the fact that, in a unique way, he is the origin, acting out of his own fullness and answering for himself. Those who hear him can entrust themselves to him for life or death, good or ill, in terms of what we call "faith". Not only would they be right in doing so, they are altogether justified in doing so. The problem of faith is not just that of having to submit to him who makes the revelation: it is the problem of finding him about whom we can be confident that he is equal to the task of proving in the long run that he really is the one in whom we have believed. We trust Jesus. He is equal to taking charge of life and existence.

Within the brief statement, "I am", or "thou art", or "he is", lies hidden everything that can be predicated of a man. But the statement is not true of Jesus in the same sense as it is of other men.

That is why absolutely everything is different when applied to him. He is made of the same stuff of life as we are: he eats, sleeps, dresses, rejoices, sorrows, travels, talks, lives and dies; and yet everything has a basically different character, by virtue of a distinction constantly at work which we have no hope of grasping directly but which may be gradually narrowed down. There is nothing miraculous about all this; yet everything is turned upside-down and transformed.

His whole existence is a "marvel", an intrusion into the world's framework, so that we can say: Such a life is impossible according to all known earthly standards. This leads us to a broader consideration. His existence is a sign, a proclamation of the divine, an epiphany. This is the import of that saying reported several times by St John: ". . . that I am he". Thus he tells his enemies (John 8. 28): "When you shall have lifted up the Son of man, then shall you know that I am he." Clearly the evangelist is acknowledging the epiphany of the Lordship of Christ: "We saw his glory, the glory as it were of the only-begotten of the Father" (John 1. 14).

2. HIS ACHIEVEMENT

Jesus is a person in a different way from us. It is not only a matter of degree: he is different in an absolute sense. It is not simply that he was more clear-minded, had greater will-power, was morally better, or of greater religious fervour. The person in him which said "I" is another—and indeed, with reference to God, other than we are. He belongs, and belongs in a way we can only call extravagant, to God, exists from him, to him and with him.

In this fact is rooted, not only the unique dignity, but also—if the word may be used—the "achievement" of Jesus.

The value of his *being-in-the-world* is determined not by what he said or did or by what happened to him, but

by what he is. More precisely, by the manner of his
being; the manner of his being himself. It is only this
that imparts their real significance to his words, his
actions, his sufferings.

All of what we can say about a man is supported and
determined by that essential content of significance indicated by the word "I". The special force which this
word has in Jesus determines the virtue and value of
his life.

Above all, this means that the whole personal life of
Jesus is unique: not just stronger, more highly developed, more intelligible, but different in quality from
other lives.

When he used the word "I" it contained no element
of that "*it*" that causes the *I* to be absorbed in the
anonymity of universal human nature; no element of
the *one*, which would submerge the *I* in the imper-
sonality of the crowd; not even an element of the *we* in
which every *I*, in spite of its essential individuality, is
inevitably involved in itself and again as the *I* of the
moment, and which is the basis for counting the un-
countable. Jesus' "I" is truly and completely *I*, in all
the uniqueness, insistence and inimitability which the
word signifies.

As a result he is capable of addressing men exactly
and of being addressed without the slightest risk of confusion with another.

He can defend to the utmost the cause of what is
based on this *I*; nothing escapes this responsibility;
nothing merely passes through the *I* or "occurs" in it.
He is equal to the responsibility, desires it and does not
relinquish it. He will not fail either through weakness
or through *hubris*.

In essence he is the one who has been "sent": to the world as a whole, to existence as such. Jesus nowhere has a private character, or a personal work of his own to do—not even in the sense in which the most duty-bound worker has it. He is never concerned with upholding his own honour.

Nor is he in the slightest degree concerned with his own good. It is important for us to observe that in Jesus' mind there is not the slightest concern about his personal welfare: he cares only for his mission. This mission is not just one task among others in the world. In essence it has the whole world for its object, the leading of all existence back home.

Hence his responsibility is towards all creatures, and he is capable of carrying out this responsibility.

Because of this, too, Jesus' experiences and trials assume a peculiar character of their own.

There are several ways by which hardship can be alleviated. One can attack or ward off the thing which threatens: shut oneself up against it or flee from it; talk it out of one's consciousness by some kind of suggestive hypnosis: confine it within certain superficial layers of pain, and so on. The most effective technique is no doubt to sidestep it inwardly, or capitulate before it, jump right into it, or in some way or other adopt an impersonal attitude and let the thing pass beside or over one.

The ultimate question is: Does the man remain *himself* through everything? Whether he does not tells us nothing about the intensity of the experience, the liveliness of the imagination, the tenderness of the feelings—all things that depend on the nature of each individual. It does, however, tell us a great deal about the *character* of his bearing under hardship, whatever be the temperament that determined this bearing. The distinction is made clear, for example, by the different ways in which the child and the adult endure pain. The child perhaps feels it more severely because he does not see beyond the present moment so that the whole of his life span is filled with the pain. The adult, on the contrary, rich in his experiences, stands firm with the determination of the mature man—in so far as he is one; for adulthood is not merely a matter of age but also, and principally, of moral depth and spiritual maturity.

Here we have an analogous experience, though on a different plane. The experience of Jesus is that of an adult and has a depth by comparison with which every man we know is but a child—unless it be that the fact of sin, with its inveterate hardness of heart and unfeelingness, demand that we give a different explanation.

V

THE UTTER OTHERNESS OF JESUS

1. THE ABSOLUTE OTHERNESS AFFIRMED

IT is now maintained with almost dogmatic certainty that the original Jesus did not claim to be more than a mere man like other men. The claim to divinity is said to have first arisen in the minds of the faithful whose community life felt the need of a figure to worship. To provide this they deified the simple Jesus of history and out of him made the Christ of faith.

Meanwhile, it is said, hidden factors were at work, seeking to tone down the claims of Jesus. "I am what you are too; so, do what I do. I am the first to be called; now I pass the call on to you : follow in my footsteps." The faithful are said to have substituted a new relationship for this one. The new idea was : "You are a different sort of being from us. You are God, and worship is your due. We are not able to do the things which you could do. We call upon you, and do you bring about in us that redemption which we are not in a position to accomplish by our own effort in God's sight." The New Testament "theologians", Paul and John, formulated this idea, it is said, and refashioned the picture of Jesus in terms of it. Does this make sense?

What St Paul says about the "Lord of Glory" (1 Cor. 2. 8); the quality and significance which the prefaces of the Epistles to the Colossians and to the Ephesians assign to the eternal Son of God; the manner in which the First Epistle to the Corinthians sees the mystical "Body of Christ" as the centre of Christian life; what Jesus says in the great discourses of St John's Gospel regarding his relationship to the Father; what the Prologue has to say about the Logos—are all these things really nothing but the inventions of a later metaphysics which obscured the original simple figure of Jesus, altering the meaning of his person and his mission?

We have already noticed how this supposedly purely human figure, in fact, defies psychology, once we refrain from explaining away its stature; and that we can sense that it possesses a centre of life which eludes all comprehension. Does this not suggest a line of thought which may lead to the possibility of decisive statements? And do not such statements actually follow in fact? And do they not arise from an awareness of an apparently—I emphasize apparently—"simple", original Jesus, and not in the least from a theological elaboration? So then, might not the Pauline-Johannine "metaphysic" be, in truth, nothing but the unfolding of what had been experienced; of what the disciples had seen, namely, the "glory of the only-begotten of the Father" (John 1. 14)?

In the preamble to his First Epistle, St John says: "That which was from the beginning, which we have heard, which we have seen with our eyes, which we have looked upon and our hands have handled, of the word of life; for the life was manifested: and we have seen and do bear witness and declare unto you the life eternal, which was with the Father and hath appeared to us: that which we have seen and have heard, we declare unto you, that you also may have fellowship with us and our fellowship may be with the Father and with his Son Jesus Christ" (1 John 1. 1–3). What are these words but the original reliable witness of this experience?

Several such statements, leading on from a supposedly purely human Jesus to the Christ of the supposed cult mysticism, are to be found in the Synoptic Gospels.

Three are of special importance: the jubilant redemptive cry of Jesus in the eleventh chapter of St Matthew; the discourse on the Last Judgement in the twenty-fifth chapter of the same Gospel; and the words uttered at the institution of the Eucharist, recorded by all the Synoptic authors.

We must examine each of these more closely.

The first passage is in St Matthew:

"At that time, Jesus answered and said: I confess to thee, O Father, Lord of heaven and earth, because thou hast hid these things from the wise and prudent, and hast revealed them to little ones. Yea, Father; for so hath it seemed good in thy sight. All things are delivered to me by my Father. And no one knoweth the Son, but the Father: neither doth any one know the Father, but the Son and he to whom it shall please the Son to reveal him. Come to me, all you that labour and are burdened, and I will refresh you. Take up my yoke upon you and learn of me, because I am meek, and humble of heart: and you shall find rest to your souls. For my yoke is sweet and my burden light" (11. 25–30).

This is a solemn declaration set forth in three stages.

The first (25–6) takes as its starting-point the apparent contradiction that yawns like a chasm between the appearance and the lack of success of Jesus, on the one hand, and his consciousness of the significance of his person and mission, on the other. But this is the very thing which demonstrates the truth, for there has to be

such a contradiction. The matter at issue is the redemption of a world enslaved to itself, in rebellion against the
holiness of God. This redemption can be effected only
by this world's being driven back within its own bounds.

The "wise" and "prudent", i.e. those who hold the
world's standards, turn away; the "children" pay heed.
To them God reveals himself in the work which he performs through Jesus. This is none other than the work
of redemption which arises from God's gracious will
and is in harmony with his good pleasure. Then (verse
27) the mighty words concerning Jesus' relationship to
the Father: the biblical "knowing", the holy, communing together face to face understanding of Father and
Son.

Besides Jesus, no one else has ever had this "knowledge", just as no one else has possessed the holy power
which is its obverse. Knowledge and authority have
been delegated to him. He gives them "to whom he
will". The freedom of disposal which lies in the Father's
good pleasure is transmitted to Jesus. An *I-Thou* relationship appears: an agreement in sovereignty. From
all this it follows that this Sonship is something other
than the sonship that is the portion of those who say the
Our Father.

The third section, however (28–30), has the
tremendous summons: "Come to me, all . . ." The
helplessness of the whole of mankind—he can deal with
it all. He brings rest. And then, equally staggering, we
hear, not of "God's", but of "my yoke"; just as in the
Sermon on the Mount he does not say "Thus saith the
Lord", but "I say to you", founded upon his: "Learn
of me, because I am meek and humble of heart." He
does, and has, and is, all that the Sermon on the Mount
requires. And he is so "from his heart"—completely,

unreservedly, with utter purity of intention. But what does this mean when we think also of another saying, such as: "If you then, being evil, know how to give good gifts to your children . . ." (Mat. 7. 11)? Does the "you" of this saying imply that all men are evil?

Here, in the straightforward language of the Synoptic Gospels, Jesus stands in a direct relationship to his Father, apart from all mankind. No man who had been brought up in the school of the Old Testament and accepted the obligations of the New could ever speak in this way. He would be putting himself outside the whole order of revelation. It would be a sacrilege against the idea of revelation as such—revolt pure and simple.

The second passage is the discourse on the Last Judgement:

"And when the Son of man shall come in his majesty, and all the angels with him, then shall he sit upon the seat of his majesty: and all nations shall be gathered together before him, and he shall separate them one from another, as the shepherd separateth the sheep from the goats: and he shall set the sheep on his right hand, but the goats on his left. Then shall the king say to them that shall be on his right hand: Come, ye blessed of my Father, possess you the kingdom prepared for you from the foundation of the world. For I was hungry, and you gave me to eat; I was thirsty, and you gave me to drink; I was a stranger, and you took me in; naked, and you covered me; sick and you visited me; I was in prison, and you came to me. Then shall the just answer him, saying: Lord, when did we see thee hungry, and fed thee, thirsty and gave thee drink? And when did we see thee a stranger, and took thee in? Or naked, and covered thee? Or when did we see thee sick or in prison, and came to thee? And the king answering shall say to them: Amen, I say to you, as long as you did it to one of these my least brethren, you did it to me. Then he shall say to them also that shall be on his left hand: Depart from me, you cursed, into everlasting fire, which was prepared for the devil and his angels. For I was hungry, and you gave me not to eat; I was thirsty and you gave me not to drink. I was a stranger, and you took me not in: naked and you covered me not: sick and in prison, and you did not visit me. Then they also shall answer him, saying: Lord, when did we see thee hungry or thirsty, or a stranger, or naked, or sick, or in prison, and did not minister to thee? Then he shall answer them, saying: Amen, I say to you, as long as you did it not to one of these least, neither did you do it to me. And these shall go into everlasting punishment: but the just, into life everlasting" (Mat. 25. 31–46).

"Judgement", in the sense of this text, is the act whereby is established the absolute truth about human existence. It is the act which removes man from his historical refusal of God, opens his heart and sets him in the presence of God. It is the act which weighs his actions and thoughts and, on this basis, confers on him his status for eternity, assigning him his eternal fate. This judgement is, therefore, an essential and non-delegable act of God.

The one who judges according to this text, however, is not "God" but Jesus. The one who sits upon the "seat of majesty" is not the God who appeared on Horeb, the unapproachable object of the prophetic theophanies, but the selfsame speaker of these words—Jesus of Nazareth. This leads inescapably to the alternative: either he knew himself to be in some manner or other the God, or, though a man, he was laying claim to the prerogatives of God.

Now, in Jesus' nature and attitude we find no trace of lust for power, arrogance or *hubris* of any sort. Anything of that nature would run counter to the deep horror of the Old Testament for any confusion between the human and the divine; would not harmonize with Jesus' own pattern of behaviour; is excluded by the limpid clarity and quintessential truth which made up his nature. It is simply impossible that Jesus could ever have let slip a word, an attitude, a spiritual gesture, capable of casting a doubt upon the exclusive divinity of God. The cleverest logician can arrive at a false conclusion; the completely just man can be deceived about his true motives; the shrewdest judge of character can be taken in by hypocrisy; but Jesus never uttered a single syllable which by implication or hidden meaning violated the honour of God. If anyone thinks that such a thing could have happened, he has not really studied Jesus.

The same demonstration is arrived at by the following question: How does Jesus judge? What are his standards? Clearly, the rule of love—in its supreme form as love of one's neighbour—but which, in accordance with the "first and greatest commandment", is the same thing as love of God.

On these terms, the judgement, according to the usual ethical norms, would be made as follows: "You, on this side, have shown love to your fellow man. God recognizes this and pronounces it to be the foundation of an eternal life of bliss for you. You, on that side, have not shown love." This fact is made known and the sentence of eternal damnation is pronounced. But this is not what happens: what is said is this: "I was in need of love; you gave it to me. You others denied it me." This does not mean simply that he, the first-called, was anticipating the objection that love had been denied only to this or that loved one, and was assuring the solidarity of all mankind by declaring that he, the Master, was one with "the least of these my brethren". Something quite different is happening here. Jesus says: To show love is to love me. To fail in love is to fail me.

What determines good and evil in the Christian scheme, what decides the value of an act in God's sight and its significance for everlasting life, is not, as in the common view of ethics, the ethical category, but he himself—his person. At the precise point in a moral act where, according to other systems, there is revealed in any concrete situation the ethical goodness of that act, here it is Christ who appears. The rational argumentation which is the basis for every moral judgement and which points to a norm (e.g. an action is good because it actualizes truth), in the Christian view, leads to his person. We do not say: This language is good because it announces the truth; we say: It is good because it affirms him—Jesus.

All this means the same thing as what the supposedly late theology of the Prologue to St John's Gospel tries to convey with its notion of the Logos. It is said there that he is the creative truth of God; that the eternal meaning of life is decided by our attitude towards him. There is, therefore, in the ethical and practical sphere, an exact analogy with the Logos idea in the metaphysical and ontological sphere.

The third passage has to do with the institution of

the Eucharist (Mat. 26. 26–8; Mark 14. 22–5; Luke 22. 19-20; 1 Cor. 11. 23–5). In St Matthew it runs thus: "And whilst they were at supper Jesus took bread and blessed and broke and gave to his disciples and said: Take ye and eat: THIS IS MY BODY. And taking the chalice, he gave thanks and gave to them, saying: Drink ye all of this. FOR THIS IS MY BLOOD OF THE NEW TESTAMENT, WHICH SHALL BE SHED FOR MANY UNTO RE-MISSION OF SINS."

To begin with, we are reading about a ritual meal which is being celebrated in commemoration of the deliverance from the bondage of Egypt and the inauguration of the theocracy in the Covenant of Sinai (Ex. 12. 1 ff.). On this action a new action is grafted. Following the original closely, we have a new institution made with a new fullness of authority, a new sacrifice, a new covenant arising out of this; a new spiritual food; a new liturgical tradition with a corresponding authority to maintain it. The whole thing is a memorial of a new event which is decisive for all time to come.

The content of all this is not some action performed by God purely and simply, a display of divine power intelligible in the context of sacred history; it is the person, the act, the destiny of him who institutes it, Jesus himself.

Furthermore, in assessing the meaning of the Eucharistic celebration we must take account of the frame of mind of the participants. They were men of ancient times who did not think in terms of abstractions, but pictorially. They were not men of Hellenistic culture ready to attach a character of divinity to anything and everything; they were men schooled in the Old Testament, with a horror of any violation of the majesty of God, of anything sensual and dionysian, men intolerant in their rejection of any semblance of mystery religion or mythology.

The act contains a statement about Christ which once again gives us an equivalent of the Logos idea. What was said about Jesus in the Prologue to St John in a metaphysical way, and by the discourse on the Last Judgement in a moralistic way, is expressed here in terms of liturgy and cult.

The following consideration underlines this. The founder says: "Take ye and eat, this is my body . . . Drink ye all of this. For this is my blood." We are not dealing here with any mere symbol of friendship or spiritual fellowship or sharing in grace, but with the very clear concept of eating and drinking. What St Paul says in 1 Corinthians, and St John reports in the discourse at Capharnaum (Chapter 6), represents a theological elaboration of what is reported by St Matthew and the others. Jesus explains unequivocally that the new existence which he preaches and makes possible is to be nourished on his own actual life. To put it negatively: in him there is nothing which is harmful, poisonous, destructive; positively: the new life of the redeemed is built up on his life.

No other man dares to speak thus. No Old Testament figure—no prophet would ever have dreamt of doing so. Nor would any New Testament figure either. No one who was caught up in the spirit and ethos of the New Testament, or who had in any way assimilated its thought, would have done so—the latter least of all. The more deeply a person becomes "Christian", the further removed is he from any disposition which might suggest that he use such language.

Our final result is, therefore, the same alternative as we noticed earlier.

These three passages which are so revealing about the suprahuman consciousness of Jesus do not stand alone, however. They merely point out very clearly what is shown in many other places by the words and deeds of Jesus. They cannot be eliminated, therefore. If they were removed, his whole figure, the whole shape of his character and thought would be destroyed.

What then is the upshot? If Jesus is a mere man, then he must be measured by the message which he brought to men. He must himself do what he expects of others; he must himself think according to the way he demanded that men think. He must himself be a "Christian".

Very well then; the more he is like that, the less he will speak, act or think as he in fact did; and the more he will be appalled by the blasphemy of the way he did behave.

If Jesus is mere man as we are, even though a very profound one, very devout, very pure—no, let us put it another way: the measure of his depth, devotion, purity, reverence, will be the measure in which it will be impossible for him to say what he says in our three passages.

The following clear-cut alternative emerges: either he is—not just evil, for that would not adequately describe the case—either he is deranged, as Nietzsche became in Turin in 1888; or he is quite different, deeply and essentially different, from what we are.

2. JESUS' ORIGINALITY

So far we have considered and tried to understand the personality of Jesus to the extent of our very limited abilities in the way one can consider and understand the greatest of human personalities. Now we must gather our findings together and complete the picture. But all we can say is that there is no such thing as a psychology of Jesus. We cannot do with him what we can do with any other man, i.e. understand him in terms of our general knowledge of the life of the human soul, determine his inner spiritual structure from an observation of his speech and behaviour, his actions and destiny; discover from such observations what alterations have taken place in him in the course of his life, what is innate in him and what are acquired characteristics, and so on. In this way we can form a picture of the nature and life of any man, and the picture is more detailed and sharper in outline the more acute our observation, the more vivid our appreciation of that person's context and background, the greater our powers of correlation. And this possibility is intensified when the observer is not detached but approaches the object of his inquiry with sympathy and love, or, it may even be to a certain degree, with hatred, for this, too, sharpens the insight.

The personality of many men is easily discernible. Others are more complicated. And then there are the contradictory, the abnormal, the morbid types. But psychological analysis is always possible, even with unusual men. Sometimes, indeed, the latter are particularly good subjects for analysis—provided the observer is competent. There is only one sphere, it would seem, which is barred to such analysis, the sphere in which the person *is* in himself and stands before God. This, however, leads us beyond our present inquiry.

No such psychology of Jesus is possible. And yet we

must be cautious. Obviously some kind of psychological understanding of him is possible because he possesses true humanity. Reading the story of the temptation, for example, and learning that he felt hungry, we see the connection between this event and the preceding fast. We understand the tension which resulted from this and the use made of it by the subsequent temptation. But who would attempt to give a final answer to the question of what hunger really meant for Christ? The reality of the elementary need, the power to work a miracle, and the refusal to use this power for his own ends; the superiority of his inner attitude, the composure of his resistance, the absence of any kind of struggle or over-excitement; the relationship of his hunger and of the whole event in general to his existence as a whole; what are we to say about all these things in the last analysis?

We read about how he loved mankind, took children into his arms and had compassion on the suffering, how he was fond of his disciples, permitting one of them to be called "the disciple whom Jesus loved", how Mary Magdalen was specially close to him, all these things obviously make some kind of "psychology" possible in his case. Our own experience and observation of every-day life help us to have some kind of understanding, to discern points of contact, to feel admiration, joy and reverence. But, taking a comprehensive view, do we understand what love really meant to Jesus? What his love was like; how did it affect him personally? If we refuse to think of Jesus either sentimentally or in terms of rationalist ethics, if we set aside the banalities of popular scientific and not-so-scientific representations, and try to see him as the Scriptures describe him, we soon realize that this love is a mystery.

Who is able to say—even with the help of every known historical and psychological factor in the conduct of religious man—that he understands what happened in the upper room at the Last Supper? Can he understand this love and self-giving, this perfect self-possession, this freedom from all strain and this tremendous purpose of giving himself to be the food of his own people? We could understand it well enough, if we were considering a pathological case: we would have the appropriate syndrome to guide us. But what can we make of him to whom the word "sick" is totally inapplicable? Anyone who says that he does understand does not know what understanding means.

We can try to enter into the hour spent in Gethsemane by employing the notion of a religious genius, interpreting the event as a state of depression; we can try to interpret his demeanour on the cross as religious fanaticism with its catastrophic turn, or again in terms of the wise man victorious over the world and using this means of testifying to his teaching. All this would yield important and interesting results; but it would not be Jesus about whom we were speaking.

In Jesus there are psychological elements, for in body and soul he is a man. The contacts spread out in all directions with their varying contents and laws. We can recognize them, but can follow them only so far and no further. In the end they withdraw into a core of mystery where our gaze cannot penetrate. And even if we study closely what is apparent, still we cannot fully understand, because this part, too, has a character which defies analysis. There is no character plan or psychological structure, no type, no biography, of Jesus. Anything which claims to be such a thing is mere muddle or deceit, for often behind the alleged analysis lurks the desire to humanize him.

Jesus cannot be dissected psychologically. He cannot be understood in terms of what we know about the nature of man; we cannot lay him bare or "get to the bottom of" him (how appropriate is that phrase). All this is what we mean when we speak of his originality.

Nor can we deduce Jesus from historical or sociological premises. Every man can be set in his historical perspective: we can show how his life has been determined by preceding and contemporary historical circumstances in the political, economic and intellectual spheres. We correlate all the data: how current ideas and literary opinions are reproduced in him; his relation to his environment, family, friends, work, social group, nationality; how his emotional life and his ideas are conditioned by all these things, and so on. And having taken account of all that he has received from his environment and from history—not forgetting the way, too, in which he has reacted *against* it, often itself an inverted sign of dependence—what is left as the man himself? Little, often so very little that we might think that individuality is nothing but a slight variation in the elements common to all life, or that it consists in the fact that it is, in a given case, this person and no other who exists in the common stuff of human life. Again, such a deduction from environment and history is quite impossible with Jesus.

It is true that he lived in a certain environment and bore its impress. He was dressed in the garb of any itinerant preacher of his time. His food, shelter, customs were those of his neighbour. For example, when we hear that he reclined at table for the Last

Supper, we can picture how he did this from the information supplied by literary and archaeological
records. He belonged to a historical period, spoke the
language of his time, used its imagery and ideas. Previous history, that is, the history of Old Testament revelation and the involvement of the people in it, were
normative for him as for his contemporaries, and historical study takes pains, indeed, to examine these factors. But how far are they operative?

Granted: Jesus is involved in his environment. But
every sentence of the Gospel story shows that he was by
no means absorbed by it. It was not only that he resisted
it, as does every man of moral earnestness when he ob-
serves false influences at work in his environment, or
every unusual man when he detaches himself from his
surroundings. His detachment from his environment
was much more fundamental. Those who encountered
him felt a basic strangeness in his nature. They do not
know quite how they stand with him. He disturbs and
startles them. Again and again it is apparent how they
are shattered, shaken in their accepted manner of
thought by him. They try to fit him into their ordinary
scheme of things, but they never succeed. This happens
not in the way it does, to some extent, with every genius
who towers above his age: it has to do with an essential
transcendence. As soon as we, in our turn, try to gain a
better insight into his nature, we become aware that
we too will fare no better. He would be alien in any
environment; in educated Hellenistic society, with the
cosmopolitan Romans, or with ordinary people. It was
not people of certain given cultural or psychological
qualities who were ready to accept him, but they who
possessed the disposition which culminates in faith.

This does not consist, however, in certain specific pre-requisites, but in a free opening up of the heart and will—and in the refusal of the forces of grace to be repulsed.

The same thing applies to history. He is in history, in the history of his people like any other man. He is part of a historical heritage—as the name "Son of David" implies. He accepts this as his own, takes up the responsibilities before God which it entails, carries it out to its logical fulfilment in his own destiny. But he does all this in a way which drives him into an ever deeper isolation than he would have known had he detached himself from it. This isolation is seen in the time he spent in the wilderness, in his hours of prayer on mountain tops, or in Gethsemane. None can "watch with" him there. This is not a question of simple material solitude, but of a qualitative, absolute solitude. "My father who is in heaven"—the "we" of the Our Father—"My Father and your Father". This, however, is the way in which he annuls history, breaks its spell and inaugurates something transformed and new. He is obedient unto death to history, in which he sees the Father's will to lie: but even here too he demonstrates that he is Lord of history. This is expressed in his essential consciousness that he is its judge—and this means something much more than that an outstanding man is judging history or altering its course. It is inseparable from his eschatological consciousness of being the judge of the world, in other words, from the Parousia. This is not some sort of crowning statement superadded to something normal; it reveals what has been inherent in his thought all along.

The fact that Jesus cannot be analysed in terms of his environment and history—things that provide the key to a very great part of every other man's nature—is indicative of his "originality".[1]

Jesus gives rise neither to an idea nor to a myth. The "idea" is a picture of the nature of a thing or of a relation. When we see an act of true courage and its special quality makes a deep impression on our minds and emotions, we know *what* courage is. The nature of courage is revealed to us. This constitutes the *idea*. It is evidenced by a particular manifestation, but it itself is more than this. When the mind grasps it, it understands the particular courageous act, but at the same time it has access to all types and grades of courageous behaviour, for there are very many of these. There are those that are obvious, those that are hidden, those that are spontaneous, those that are performed only after self-discipline, those that are magnanimous, those that are grudging, and so on. Whoever has once grasped the idea of courage is able to appreciate it in its various

[1] The category of originality is rooted in one of the prime questions of being: in the question of origin. It plays a prominent part in early mythological thoughts. All primitive theogonies and cosmogonies are an answer to the question where everything comes from; about that which itself has no beginning, but gives existence to all else, furnishing all things with life and energy. The question about beginning—about the *arche*—is the first systematic question arising from the impression made on us by what is, the impression that it does not exist of itself, but is in a state of flux; that it does not explain itself, but points back to something else. Wonder then gives way to philosophical inquiry and evokes the counterquestion: where is everything going? From these two questions arises man's predicament, theoretical and existential. Everything comes from the origin—endowment, achievement, destiny. This, too, receives a philosophical and scientific elaboration. The question of both ultimates affects everything. Here we have to do with one of the *schemata* of all investigation, perhaps the most fundamental of all: originality.

embodiments, and able to judge it and assess its importance for life as a whole.

Does such an idea of Christ exist? There have been
those who affirm that it does, and they have claimed to
be able to expound it—the idea of pure humanity or
perfect goodness or total attachment to God. Since the
Enlightenment there has been a tendency to see things
in the light, and, as a result, his nature has been cor-
roded and finally eaten away.

Again, men have probed deeper and said that the
relevant idea was that of the God-man. At first, this
would seem to be a brighter suggestion. But if there is
an idea of the God-man, it must be one we can grasp
just like every other idea, through experience, reflection and inner illumination: in the world around us
and within our minds. What would the God-man idea
mean on these terms? Something highly ambiguous:
divinity, as we imagine it to be: humanity, as we know
it; both united in a way familiar to us, in some such
way as body and soul are united, or as consciousness is
related to the basic thought that determines it, or as the
first rung in the ladder of evolution is related to its
highest peak. Whatever emerged would be something
highly contradictory, highly heterogeneous, in which
everything, the divine and the human, and the connection between them, would be spoiled. Beings of this
kind, in fact, have often been thought of—imagined
would be a better word—in the case of the ancient
demigods and heroes, the superhuman geniuses of the
Renaissance and the ideal figures of eighteenth-century
classicism, the demigod of Hölderlin, and the superman
of Nietzsche. But Christ has no part in any of these.
When we hear it said that he is the God-man, we learn
nothing at all about him which our experience of this

world enables us to understand. The term means that he is something qualitatively new and different, which receives its meaning only from the inner life of God himself, and from God's conception of and plan for man.

A myth of Christ is lacking too, as well as an idea of him. Myths are forms and incidents which arise in the primitive contemplative and pictorial mind and by which it expresses the nature of the world and its own existence. The mythology of the sun, for example, tells us about a mighty supernatural being of light who rises in majesty and conquers the dragon darkness, bringing light, warmth and fertility. In the course of battle with the dragon he is, however, defeated; but only in the end to rise anew. This myth is descriptive both of the soul and its desire for light and of the fate which befalls it. Its expression is found in the various sun gods, and in the sagas of heroes like Siegfried and Krishna.

Christ is in no sense the embodiment of a myth of this kind. In no sense can we interpret him in terms of the power and the destiny of light, or in terms of any other myth motif such as that of fertility, which springs from the marriage of heaven and earth. This is ruled out by the very obvious fact that he is an historical person. The mythical figures are related to history like the horizon which ever recedes as we approach it, but Christ stands right in the middle of history, at a clearly defined point in time, space, and historical sequence. Take his whole figure, his attitude, his actions, his relationship to God and to man: none of this shows the slightest trace of the idealization which is characteristic of the myth, a thing that is universal and yet never existed. He is the very opposite of the myth, full of symbolism but making no obligatory demands on anyone. He is completely nonideal and non-symbolic. He is through and through reality itself. He is a person and speaks to other persons. Hence that realism, that almost banal everyday quality about him, which has enabled the metaphysicians and the mythomaniacs to feel superior with regard to him. But it is he who sets the person in motion and gives reality to life. His nature is completely lacking in all the paganism which is so characteristic of the myth, all the worldliness, and all the inability to rise above the things of this world which we find in the myth. He shatters every mythology and brings men through all that is tinged by the world that hinders a relationship with a personal, holy God. Thus we can understand why all the myth lovers instinctively hate everything that he represents.

The fact that there is neither an idea nor a myth which discloses the nature of Jesus is a further indication of his originality.

We can sum all this up by saying: There exists no *concept* of Jesus. A *concept* is the expression of an intelligible reality. A concept is what human thinking attains when it has managed to become master of an object by abstracting it from the conditions in which it exists in the world. It is the general symbol under which the particular is subsumed. Of Christ there can be no such concept.

Of him we have only a name—the name which God himself gave him. The words "Jesus Christ" do not connote any general idea but express one single, particular occurrence. They are the name of him who once came among us and suffered a death which was our redemption. He alone can reveal what he is.

There is a parallel between one of the most important

passages in the Old Testament and Jesus' mighty saying
about himself. The former is in Exodus, in the account
of God's revelation on Mount Horeb. There Moses saw
the bush burning without being consumed, and in the
flames there appeared the form of the "angel of the
Lord", God's emissary, who was at the same time God
himself. From him Moses received a commission to lead
the people out of bondage. Then Moses asks: "Lo, I
shall go to the children of Israel, and say to them: The
God of your fathers hath sent me to you. If you should
say to me: What is his name? What shall I say to them?
God said to Moses: I AM WHO AM. He said: Thus shalt
thou say to the children of Israel: HE WHO IS hath sent
me to you" (Ex. 3. 13–14). Here God reveals his name.
And what is this name? Strictly speaking, it is a declin-
ing to accept definition in terms of anything belonging
to the world. It is a claim to complete sovereignty over
everything in the world. At the same time it is a claim
to possess the fullness of intelligence and being, and a
claim that this fullness springs entirely from him alone
and is entirely in him alone. This is the divinity of God
which arouses in the man who is attuned to it a response
of adoration.

In St John's Gospel we are told how Jesus was dis-
puting with his enemies, and said to them: "I am he"
(8. 28). These words are language which only God could
use. They express the same thought as was expressed on
Horeb. Jesus "is he", purely and simply. He is the one
who counts; the one through whom the redemption is
accomplished; the one in whom the new creation
originates. And so, when Christ says in the Apocalypse:
"I am Alpha and Omega, the first and the last, the beginning and the end" (22. 13), he is only enlarging upon
this little sentence.

Truly, he came into this world and entered into history, a man with a man's body and soul. But he was there in a manner, and was real in a manner that eludes every human concept.

In the genuineness of his incarnation he belongs to this world, but at the same time he is independent of it. As such he addresses the world, lifts it out of its falseness, and sets it on a new path, grants it a fresh start—and he himself is its beginning.

This is what determines man's relationship to Christ. The act by which he comes to Christ, and the relationship with him upon which he enters, must share in Christ's own character. The props provided by the various certainties he finds in the things of the world are all lacking. Christ is the beginning, the subjective beginning, the beginning of life; and one only reaches this beginning by actually beginning.

There are certain approaches, it is true: the longing for redemption; the search for a liberating leadership; the questions: where from, where to, why and wherefore? When a man who is thus prepared meets Christ, he realizes: I can trust him; here is "the way, the truth, and the life". Something in him, Tertullian's *anima naturaliter christiana*, recognizes in Christ him who has come. But all this is, as we said, but an approach. The step itself, which constitutes making a start, must be freely made.

In Christ there begins that which is genuinely new; thus there is no pathway leading from the world to him on which we shall not need daring in order to overcome the hazard represented by the "rock of offence": by the feeling that we may be "making fools of ourselves".

At this point, then, it is quite clear that our description has left something out of the total picture: the thing which enables a man to dare all and throw himself upon Christ. We will have to say: That beginning which is Christ himself evokes a beginning in man—liberates it, nay, creates it. The beginning in man is the echo of the beginning, which is Christ.

The beginning which appeared corporeally in the world in Christ, and the beginning which he creates in man, form a unity. Christ has come as our Redeemer, in love. This means he came to us and "for us". And so, if we may express it thus, his Redeemership is for ever fulfilled and accomplished in the response given by man whom he calls, to whom he offers the possibility of entering into the new beginning and thus beginning himself.

All this is what is called "grace". Man is to recognize Christ, decide for him, come to him, dare all for him, make a new start from him—and yet, all the time, this is the effect of action already taken on God's side and forms a unity with that which is in Christ.

The act, thus elicited by grace and directed towards Christ, in which all that is most individual in man's nature finds its true realization, although it is entirely invitation and free gift, is faith. Faith, on the human side, is the actualization of that beginning which Christ effects through his whole being.

In all this a decision—*the* decision *simpliciter*—is required. The various attempts to see Jesus in a psychological or sociological or mythological sense all end up in the same way: they shy away from the decision and give us nothing but considerations on universal humanity. However important or interesting this universal humanity may be, it is, in fact, a secondary thing. The man who makes these attempts does not see the Jesus who originates in the freedom of God at all, but himself remains imprisoned in the confines of this world. Jesus is truly seen only by the man who believes in him, or who—and this is the real antithesis of faith—finds him a stumbling-block.

Jesus said so himself. He answered the Forerunner's question: "Art thou he that is to come, or look we for another?" in such a way as to apply Isaiah's prophecy to himself and to make plain that it was being fulfilled in him, i.e. that he was the Messiah. Then he added: "And blessed is he that shall not be scandalized in me" (Mat. 11. 3, 6). The possibility that people would be scandalized by him was part of his nature, for the very reason that he is the beginning. He expected men to give up the certainties of this world and risk everything for his sake. If a man was able to accept these terms, then the new relationship of grace and of faith emerged and a new life began. But if the man shut up his heart and refused, then he rebelled against the notion that Christ was expecting this of him; and this constitutes being scandalized.

Faith or scandal: these are the only real attitudes caused in man by Christ. Faith sees him as the beginning and takes its stance there. It is prepared to think and live as from Christ, to submit to his judgement and appeal to his grace. Scandal affirms that he is the enemy of life, the world's adversary, and declares on him a war the like of which is unknown. Perhaps the only clearly defined lesson of history is to the effect that this cleavage becomes more and more pronounced. More and more obviously the world is becoming divided into those who believe in Christ and those who find him a scandal.[1]

3. JESUS' BEING COME

In what has just been written, we have discussed the *originality* of Jesus. By that was meant the fact that he cannot be deduced from the things of this world. He is not just one factor in a continuous, homogeneous succession, no matter how vast; no, in his own utter uniqueness he stands over against everything we know in this world. This is made clear by the fact that there is no psychology, no sociological or historical explanation, no idea or myth of Jesus. In this world he exists in quite another way from this world's own beings. He transcends all the concepts of the way in which what is, is.

The manner of this being must now once more be examined—and according to his own way of seeing it.

The tree we see before us in its particular form and shape came from a seed, which in turn came from a tree of the same species. Roots, stem, branches, twigs, leaves, flowers, fruit, have all formed themselves out of the stuff of earth and air which surrounds the tree. Light has affected it, the wind has moved it, the rain has moistened it. In due time the tree dies; but from its seed new trees of the same kind have already sprung up. If, then, we ask how this tree exists, how it came to be and is here now, the answer would proceed as follows: It has grown out of the combination of circumstances one must postulate when talking of trees. It comes out of

[1] On the character of this warfare, see the much repeated thought in St John's Gospel: "You desire to kill me", rising to a pitch in the desire of Jesus' enemies to kill Lazarus whom he had raised from the dead (John 12. 10).

nature as a whole and is ultimately re-absorbed by nature. It is one factor in the totality of life, or more exactly, of this particular species of tree; more exactly still, of a succession of individual trees which is made up of fruit, tree, and then fruit once more. Once this particular tree has grown and its life-span is run, it disappears again into the totality of nature.

Man is different. With him, too, there is much that has been produced: his bodily organism has come from those of his parents, his mental riches from what his environment can offer, his way of thinking from historical circumstances. Nonetheless, there is in him an essential limit which is set, for in man there is something which has not been produced: his spiritual soul. His busy mind tells him that his soul comes from somewhere else, from a realm beyond nature, bringing with it mental faculties which create between it and nature a state of tension. Religions and systems of philosophy interpret this relationship. Faith gives the final definition by saying that the soul does not arise out of the context of this world but comes, each one individually and once only, from the creative will of God. Thus each man bears a direct relationship to God. He feels his bond with the mystery of his created origin—at least he can feel it if he pays proper attention to it. This bond runs through and beyond all his relations of dependence on the world and is the foundation of his religious life. Existence begins afresh, therefore, with every man; and so the history of mankind is something quite different from the genealogy of a variety of trees or the pedigree of a breed of animals. It is, rather, a continuity, the separate parts of which are not completely contained in it, but are, each one individually, also related to God, so that they enjoy all the positive and negative advantages of being beginnings. This gives rise to the dialectic structure of history; from this, too, comes the fact that there is no ultimate finality in any historical phenomenon. There is no problem connected with existence as such, which is ever finally settled. Each man, in his own individual existence, must take them up again. This is the cause of the insecurity in history: it is for every being once more called in question. Hence, too, the ever new possibilities and fresh hope associated with each human being.

The tree has its origin within this world; man, with his spiritual soul, is projected into it. The existence of Christ is once more totally different and this time in an absolute sense. In him, too, there is a produced element: his bodily organism is derived from a human mother; he bears in himself the heritage of an ancient line; his personality harbours the common thought-heritage of the men of his time. And in Christ too there is that directly created thing: his mighty and holy soul which proceeded from the creative will of God, like the soul of each one of us. But what is most characteristic about him is something of another kind altogether. He is the Son of God and as such has "come into the world".

What is the significance of this for his existence?

The saying that he has come is very much his own; it expresses what was uppermost in his mind. "I came not to call the just, but sinners", he says in St Mark's Gospel (2. 17). In St John it forms one of the basic motifs of his presentation, and is the thing which gives this Gospel its special air of mystery. Thus Jesus says to Pilate: "For this was I born, and for this came I into the world; that I should give testimony to the truth" (18. 37). Still more impressive are his words to his dis-

ciples at the Last Supper: "I came forth from the
Father, and am come into the world: again I leave the
world, and I go to the Father" (16. 28). But the Prologue says of the Son of God: "He came unto his own,
and his own received him not" (1. 11). The opposition
of the world into which he comes serves to underline
the fact of his coming.

The saying about his "coming" is no mere manner of
speaking: it describes a fact. We sense a genuine movement; the traversing of a distance along a road, a
decision which has moved someone to make a journey,
and a place from which the journey started. The statement is most revealing. It makes it quite plain that God
is not merely absolute Spirit, existing everywhere and
maintaining all things, but that he is also he who arises,
sets out and arrives. In Christ, the Son of God exists as
he who has come into this world.

This advent is no adventure of some divine hero, but
is undertaken under commission and with power. Jesus
himself says—and the saying again expresses his most
profound consciousness of himself and his nature that
he has been "sent".

This thought, too, permeates the whole of the Fourth
Gospel: "As the Father hath sent me, I also send you"
(John 20. 21), he tells his apostles after the resurrection.

A decree lies behind his coming: the eternal decree
of the Father of which St Paul speaks in the Epistle to
the Colossians (1. 19–20): "Because in him, it hath well-
pleased the Father, that all fulness should dwell; and
through him to reconcile all things unto himself."

This decree is present throughout the life of Jesus:
it is always there when he is speaking about the Father's
will. His coming, as his entry into earthly existence, is

balanced by his fulfilment of the Father's will, his
obedience to him, as the constant determinant of his
actions. The form in which this holy will is expressed,
as it is concretely manifested through the facts of daily
existence is "his hour". "My hour is not yet come"
(John 2. 4). This direct determination by the "will"
dominates every inner and spiritual situation.

Let us repeat: the Son could only "be sent" and
"come" because he existed eternally as a living person.
He is not just some energy which emanates from the
Father: no mere enlightenment granted to a man; certainly no ethico-religious form of self-perfection or a
stage in man's mystical development: he is himself, a
true person.

The Epistle to the Hebrews expresses this fact by
saying: "Wherefore, when he cometh into the world,
he saith: . . . Behold I come. In the head of the book
it is written of me, that I should do thy will, O God"
(10. 5, 7). In St John's Gospel we read in the high-
priestly prayer: "And now glorify thou me, O Father,
with thyself, with the glory which I had, before the
world was, with thee" (17. 5). The source of this existence is finally expressed in the following text: "No man
hath seen God [the Father, that is] at any time: the
only-begotten Son who is in the bosom of the Father,
he hath declared him" (1. 18).

This is the ultimate origin. We cannot go back any
further. This is the primal realm of God to which the
Prologue to St John refers: the love within God himself, into which no created thing intrudes: "In the beginning was the Word, and the Word was with God,
and the Word [himself] was God. The same was in the
beginning with God" (1. 1–2).

This eternal Word, the eternal Son who is in the

bosom of the Father, has "come" in Christ, and is now "with us".

These three sayings are of inexhaustible meaning: *come* into the world . . . *sent* by the Father's decree . . . *born* of the Father before all ages . . . These describe the way in which Christ exists in the world.

We would do well to ponder these sayings in the depths of our soul, in order to be able to distinguish what must be distinguished: plants and animals arise out of this world; man with his personal spiritual core is projected into it; Christ comes into it from beyond. This fact determines his nature. The consciousness of this is alive in him. Therefore he is the mystery we see in him and that he is. Therefore he is at once the one whom we know and the one who is unknowable. He is truly there, but has an infinite road behind him. He is actually in the world, but in such a manner that the world can never engulf him.

He can never be explained in terms of the world, never be seen as a mere component part of it. He is for ever the one who has come. For ever it is he who gives the jolt to the world's self-assurance. He is for ever breaking through the world's self-sufficiency in its unity.

And thus, too, he departs out of this world. But there is a difference here also. The forms of trees and animals dissolve and become material from which new forms arise. Man's soul is called by its Creator and comes before him for eternal judgement. Christ goes home to his Father.

His farewell utterances are full of the mystery of this homeward journey. "Little children, yet a little while I am with you. You shall seek me, and as I said to the Jews: Whither I go you cannot come: so I say to you now" (John 13. 33). More plainly: "I go to the Father" (14. 13), "I go to him that sent me" (16. 5). And very precisely: "I came forth from the Father, and am come into the world: again I leave the world, and I go to the Father" (16. 28). The same distinction established between the concepts of being born, sent, and coming, and that of human entering on existence, appears here with regard to the way in which man departs from this earthly scene. Man dies and his soul appears before its Creator to be judged: Christ "goes to his Father", back to the primal realm of divine beginning, to that place where what he prayed for at the end of his farewell discourses is present reality: "That they all may be one, as thou, Father, in me, and I in thee: that they also may be one in us"[1] (17. 21). And again: "And now glorify thou me, O Father, with thyself, with the glory which I had, before the world was, with thee" (17. 5).

Jesus' existence in this world, therefore, is different from ours. It is a coming and a returning. It is a passing through, which forges through the deepest abyss of life and bears everything up into the holy beginning of the redemption and new creation. And this beginning, no earthly or worldly context can hold it back.

If this is Christ, then the world cannot comprehend him by itself. He himself will have to supply the means for it to understand. And this is what he says himself, on several occasions: that only those will understand his words aright "who have ears to hear" (Mat. 11. 15; 13. 9, 16); that only those whom the Father helps can come to him, who stands before them in his visible,

---

[1] This "us" is a tremendous word. It appears earlier too: "We will come to him, and will make our abode with him" (14. 23).

palpable reality: "No man can come to me, except the Father, who hath sent me, draw him" (John 6. 44). St Paul repeats this idea emphatically: "No man can say the Lord Jesus, but by the Holy Ghost" (1 Cor. 12. 3). This means that no one is able to profess a real belief in the Lord as Redeemer, unless God enables him to do so.

The aim of Christ's coming is that he should arrive and be accepted. But for this he himself has to prepare the dwelling and give it the power to open up to him. This is faith.

Here we use the word "faith" in the sense which is usually given to it by the New Testament, not as a name for faith as distinguished from hope and love, as in the First Epistle to the Corinthians, or as distinguished from prayer and good works, but as the Christian act *per se*, as the response to revelation and redemption. Faith is the being struck by the coming of God in Christ: a living encounter, acceptance, union in trust and loyalty. The capacity to respond in this way is given by the very one himself who comes. If Christ were to come while men remained what they are of their own nature, none would recognize him, none would accept him. All would find him an offence, a stumbling-block, as the Prologue to St John's Gospel says: "The darkness did not comprehend it . . . his own received him not" (1. 5, 11). The same divine movement which is the Lord's coming also creates faith in the soul. His coming and our believing constitute an indivisible whole.

Thus, faith, too, is a "beginning". It does not arise from the temperament and capacities of the men who have it, nor yet from the contingencies of their environment, but is generated by God. Faith is the act of the "new life" of which the New Testament speaks. It is the sign and the proof of new birth. For example, we read in St John: "Jesus therefore said to them: If God were your Father, you would indeed love me. For from God I proceeded and came: for I came not of myself, but he sent me. Why do you not know my speech? Because you cannot hear my word. . . . If I say the truth to you, why do you not believe me? He that is of God heareth the words of God. Therefore you hear them not, because you are not of God" (John 8. 42–7).

It is true that faith contains a host of derivative elements. A man's faith life has its psychology. Certain patterns can be shown to exist in every man's life of faith; features which are connected with his family or race; others which are peculiar to the individual. We will find in it the same structure as governs his whole mental and spiritual life. A man's faith will differ from a woman's; a child's from an adult's; that of a crude person from that of a cultured person, and so on. But the essence of faith always eludes psychology. It goes back to God. It shares in the manner of Christ's own being. All faith has its social and its historical side also. The faith of the ancient world followed a different pattern from that of the Middle Ages or of modern times. In times of peace and economic and cultural development, religious life is different from what it is in times of upheaval or revolution. The man who is socially oppressed displays a different religious psychology from the man who is a member of the ruling class. But the core of faith in all these cases is always rooted in the eternal. It escapes beyond all these temporal considerations. It consists in the fact of being born of God. In the face of this fact, all mundane distinctions fade into insignificance. They are unessential. All faith has its own logic, too. The person who believes can give an account of the motives which seem convincing to him, but when all is said and done, belief eludes all logical analysis. Belief contains some of the stuff of this world, the natural energies of body and soul and human relationships. Everything that is intelligible about it belongs to the elements which this world furnishes. At the same time, however, there is alive in it that something different that is not of this world. That which was established once and for all when the Son of God became man—God's own being within creation—is consummated anew in each believer through grace and participation. Belief must be seen as an act connected with the path trodden by Christ in his coming. It is the "place", ever new, where the arrival of the Son of God is welcomed.

Faith is for Christ as the eye is for the light. It is determined by him who effected the incarnation as well —by the Holy Spirit. It is man's movement in response to the movement of the Redeemer. It is the obverse of his coming, related to it as love is to love, and only together with it forming the totality of the new life.

Faith is, if we may say so, the same sort of thing as Christ. It is in the world as Christ was: as a starting-point. It is in the world but not of it. It neither derives from the world nor merges into it. It has a duty towards it but is never its slave. It knows more about the world than the world knows about itself. It carries in itself the world's destiny more deeply than the world itself ever can; and yet it is raised above the world and is alien to it. This is what St John really expresses when he says: "This is the victory which overcometh the world: our faith" (1 John 5. 4).

And so the world looks upon every true believer as it looks upon Christ: as a stumbling-block; not as some object to be considered, understood and appraised but as a "sign that shall be contradicted" (Luke 2. 34). In all who encounter him, the true believer evokes either love or hate: ultimately, either faith or the desire to destroy.

And faith follows the pattern of Christ's existence in this too, that it cannot justify itself by compulsion in this world. The moment the world shuts up its heart, faith appears to be "foolishness", and its only course is to appeal to judgement. But the judgement is beyond the grave. Hence the appeal is difficult, for it has to be made and maintained in spite of its appearance of having been disallowed.

4. JESUS AS TEACHER, AS POWER, AS HE WHO IS

In what figures can we best sum up what the New Testament has to say about the person of Christ in general, his words, his deeds and his fate?

First of all, in that of the holy teacher.

He has the fullness of the knowledge of God. Not only does he know more than anyone else, he also knows it in another way: through living vision and being. He knows man and the world. Men are blinded by sin; he sees. He distinguishes reality from appearance, truth from deception. He knows good and evil. He knows the way. And his knowledge is clear and of his essence. Thus he had the power of words: "The people were in admiration at his doctrine. For he was teaching them as one having power; and not as the scribes" (Mat. 7. 28-9). This shows Christ as the teacher *par excellence*, in whose words holy and pure truth resides.

But he did more than just teach. He acted in accordance with his teaching. His attitude of mind, his relationship to God, his whole life was behind his words. He
was able to ask his enemies: "Can any of you convict
me of sin?" (John 8. 46); and to say: "Follow me" (Mat.
4. 19; 8. 22; 9. 9; Mark 2. 14; Luke 9. 59; John 1. 43;
21. 19, 22).

This is the picture of the reality which is Christ that
men from time immemorial have found easiest to
accept. This fact is connected with the pre-eminent
place occupied by knowledge in human life generally
and in the prevailing cultural climate of the Middle
Ages and modern times. But this does not tell us all or
even the most important thing of all. The crux of the
matter lies deeper.

Standing before Pilate, Jesus said: "For this was I
born, and for this came I into the world; that I should
give testimony to the truth. Everyone that is of the
truth, heareth my voice" (John 18. 37). In his farewell
discourse he said: "I am the way, and the truth, and
the life" (14. 6). In the Prologue to St John we read:
"In the beginning was the Word, and the Word was with
God, and the Word was God. The same was in the beginning with God. All things were made by him: and
without him was made nothing that was made" (1. 1–3).
These three texts form a mighty crescendo and disclose
a relationship to truth which can be understood only
gradually. Their form, like that of all the words of
Christ recorded by John, is the fruit of long meditation.
But the latter has altered nothing, for it also was in
accordance with the apostolic commission and was carried out in the power of the Holy Spirit. St John is
looking back to "what his eyes had seen, his ears had
heard, and his hands had handled of the Word of truth"

(cf. 1 John 1. 1) and asks: Who was this? What was he like? What content and attitude of mind are expressed in his words? John gives the answers to these questions in the form of "discourses" put into the mouth of Jesus according to the historical method of the time. So these too are *kerygma*, message, proclaimed truth.

We must understand our three texts in these terms. "Truth" means that the temporal acquires its real meaning for us in an eternal perspective; that being becomes intellectually clear when it is seen in the light of the idea and the corporality of the word. *We* have to seek and to find this truth—he says: "I am" this truth. In him, being itself is seen in the clear light of truth. Not merely in that he does not lie or that he is honest, but in the way in which he exists. All that is, is like a tightly closed bud that opens up in the light of the "idea". Jesus does not discover this "idea", above himself, in eternity, the realm of meaning to which he would have to raise himself. He finds it in himself. More correctly: he is that idea. And the word, which is the means whereby mute knowledge steps out free into the open, is not just that elemental act of man which is proper even to him; it is something of a totally different nature. He himself is the creative Word who alone makes communication at all possible.

St John says just this. He describes the existence of Christ by saying: Christ is "the Logos", who was "in the beginning", that is, in eternity, before all time and change began. He was "with God", "towards God", the "Son who is in the bosom of the Father" and is "God himself", who was "made man" and was "among us", visible, audible, apparent to our senses.

This is a tremendous affirmation and it forces on us

that inescapable decision which is quite simply the mark of the truth that speaks in God's name, the truth that is essentially at once redemption and judgement. It points back to the eternal life of God; to a society within his unity, a society which has the character both of primal truth and of being the sheer foundation of all truth.

When he teaches, therefore, he is not saying something that was all ready-made though perhaps hidden: he is uttering the truth which he himself is and which is the foundation of all other truth. He is the idea which makes all things true. In the sphere and light of his words, all true statements are true.

That being so, any concept of "the teacher" which we might be able to build up from our experience is left far behind: we have gone forward to something unique.

He is also power.

By this we do not mean that he wields an external power over men like some man of action over his fellows in the social or political sphere. He could easily have exercised such power. The people were ready to proclaim him their Messiah and king. But he always refused to allow them to do so (John 6. 15). Before Pilate he said: "My kingdom is not of this world" (John 18. 36). When Peter wanted to defend him with a sword, he said: "Put up again thy sword into its place . . . Thinkest thou that I cannot ask my Father, and he will give me presently more than twelve legions of angels? How then shall the scriptures be fulfilled, that so it must be done?" (Mat. 26. 52-4).

The power he has and exercises is of a different order.

It is most tangibly seen in his miracles—as a power over the reality of things, that is; as the ability to take hold of them and place them at the direct service of the

Kingdom of God. This power, original and credible, is evident everywhere in the Gospels.

The *Fioretti* of St Francis tell how he performed one miracle after another. Most of these are probably legendary; yet the story is correct on one point: men were aware of an overwhelming holy power in Francis and expressed this in the form of the stories which show how all things bent to his will. This cannot but be the experience of all too who read the Gospels with an open heart and mind. Even if a man were not prepared to believe in the possibility of miracles, he would still sense the power conveyed by these stories, and would have to face up to the phenomenon they represent.

But the miracles of Jesus did happen. We are certain of this by faith. Each miracle is not merely a sign that Jesus helped one or cured another; it is a revelation of holy power, of that holy power of which it is written: "All power is given to me in heaven and earth" (Mat. 28. 18), the full authority, that is, of him who has been sent.

Besides this, the creative power of God which is described in the first chapters of Genesis is defined in the "Genesis of the New Testament", the Prologue to St John's Gospel: "All things were made by him [the Logos]; and without him was made nothing that was made. . . . He was in the world and the world was made by him" (John 1. 3, 10). Earlier than this it had been defined in the Epistle to the Colossians: "For in him were all things created in heaven and on earth, visible and invisible, whether thrones, or dominations, or principalities, or powers: all things were created by him and in him: and he is before all; and by him all things consist" (1. 16–17). This power manifests itself here and sets about new tasks.

There is power in his words as well. At the close of
the Sermon on the Mount, the passage we have already
quoted informs us: "And it came to pass when Jesus
had fully ended these words, the people were in admiration at his doctrine. For he was teaching them as one
having power; and not as the scribes" (Mat. 7. 28–9).
This does not mean merely that his words were strong,
bold, fired with the ardour of enthusiasm. It means
much more: his words touched the heart at a depth
beyond the reach of any human words. They removed
deceit and set men right in front of God the holy one.
They summoned everyone—even the respectable and
pious—to return to God; and they made it possible for
them to do so.

His words were not just meaningful symbols: they
were power—power from God, the power of the Holy
Spirit.

And in his gesture, too, there is power, in his actions,
and in his figure. We have heard how at the Passover he
turned all the merchants and traffickers out of the
Temple. It was the time of pilgrimage; Temple and city
were filled with excited people from all over the world.
When he drove the dealers and bargainers away from
their profits he had neither weapon nor friends to assist
him, nor did he use inflammatory speeches to set on the
mob; but with an economy of words and a few cords
twisted together he swept out the whole lot of them.
What a power must have radiated from him then! The
ancient fear of God must have broken out from him
upon the people at that moment (John 2. 13–21). Or
remember Nazareth, the time when he preached in the
synagogue. At first they marvelled at "the words of grace
that proceeded from his mouth"; then they felt the re-

proach in his words and became enraged. A paroxysm took hold of them; they dragged him up to the brow of the hill and tried to throw him down. He made no plea, spoke no word to free himself, made no attack, but, we read: "Passing through the midst of them, [he] went his way" (Luke 4. 16–30). This reveals even more power, it may be, than the event in the Temple: this emanation of a silent power, resigned in its trust in God, before which men simply give way and let him go free. Then there is the great scene in the darkness at Gethsemane: Judas comes with an armed guard and he asks: "Whom seek ye? They answered him: Jesus of Nazareth. Jesus saith to them: I am he. And Judas also, who betrayed him, stood with them. As soon therefore as he had said to them: I am he; they went backward and fell to the ground" (John 18. 4–6). This is no embroidered legend; it is the plain truth. A shock must have gone out from him—all the more amazing, considering that soon after he gave himself up and let them bind him.

This power pervaded all he was and did. It was the power of a colossal personality, of a deep recollection of soul, of a completely free will, perfectly attuned to its holy mission, in a word, the power of Presence. Behind this lay even more power, ready to burst forth from God—so immediate that, for example, after the miraculous catch of fish, when he was sitting in the ship, Peter fell at his feet in fear, crying out: "Depart from me for I am a sinful man, O Lord! For he was wholly astonished, and all that were with him" (Luke 5. 8–9). It was not just amazement, astonishment, but terror, overwhelming awe, caused by the terrible presence of God's power—the Old Testament fear of God.

Yet even this does not exhaust the matter. There is still something else to be said, and it is hard to say —perhaps impossible. We can but try to express it. The ultimate and most powerful thing is Jesus' existence.

If I say, "This is I", I mean more than simply that there are here a body, a spiritual being, various attributes, to which I attach the added precision that they belong to me and not to another. I mean not only that I have all these things, but that I also completely permeate them with my life, I make them what they are. The proposition, "I am", does not denote a fragment of reality, to which the statement that it is "I" and not another applies. No; that with which we are concerned, the reality of substance, powers and attributes, is in act, in *my* act. "I am" signifies an action : the most inward act of which I am capable, the act behind every particular action, striving, struggling, taking, walking, eating, sleeping, thinking, talking and working. It is that primal exertion by which I preserve myself from nonexistence, maintain myself in reality and thrust nothingness from me. It is an exertion which is carried on in the deepest roots of my being, and its ultimate anxiety is experienced in all those feelings—we are today acutely conscious of them—of constriction, loneliness, insecurity and fear for one's safety. When we say that a man is alive—more alive than others—we mean, in the first place, that he is more capable of experiencing things, more enterprising, more able to cope with the world than others are. True aliveness, however, lies deeper. A man can be more deprived, more oppressed, more tired than others, and still be, in the last resort, more alive than others, if there is in him less of what is superficial, of what is merely possessed; if in him, being is more awake, more in motion, more complete—in a word, is more *act*.

These considerations help us to understand better what the word "existence" means when applied to Jesus. He does not just happen to be—he "is". He is not merely made up of this and that but he "exists" it. In him the Son of God came into the world, assuming a human form, not in order to confer a favour upon it, to use it as a dwelling-place, but in order to "be" it. He penetrated this human nature in all its parts, enlightened it, sanctified it, accepted responsibility for it, dignified it utterly. This human nature had a full living experience of God, knew him, experienced him, willed him. He who said "I", "was" this unity. We cannot express it.

What a statement that was when he said: "I am"! What an act this "I am"; what a being there, standing there, self-being, self-knowledge, self-act! No battle here against non-existence, none of the pain and danger of our uncertainty—he is inviolable, Lord in Being. On Horeb Moses asked God: "What is thy name?" and God replied: "I am who am" and "I am is my name" (Ex. 3. 14). This "I am" now appears again, and St John has a saying in which is expressed the awareness that it is the same—we have already cited it elsewhere: "When you shall have lifted up the Son of Man, then shall you know that I am he" (John 8. 28). The saying of Horeb is here found on the lips of Jesus.

The final and deepest thing is then—Christ's existence. Everything else merely comes after this: the power of his words and acts; his all-embracing love; the depth of his knowledge and wisdom; his doctrine and

his example; the magnitude of all that befell him—all
these things are irradiated by that basic fact. Its consummation is Christ's life. We sense the terrifyingly
mighty stream of this self-realization flowing unseen
beneath all we see and perceive. His words and gestures
rise up out of this. It is this from which his actions and
his destiny spring. On occasion we are allowed a glimpse
into this abyss; in the temptation episode, for example,
when the adversary's onslaught glances off the monu-
mental imperturbability of this existence (Mat. 4. 1 ff.);
in the gladness when the apostles returned and he "rejoiced in spirit" at the reversal of standards in God's
sight, and called the disciples blessed, for their eyes had
been permitted to see him (Luke 10. 21–4); in the great
discourses which John reports—"Verily, verily, I say
to you, before Abraham was, I am" (8. 58), or finally, in
the last great prayer after the Last Supper, and in the
celebration of the Supper itself (John 14–17).

This deep life of Jesus may have had its various
changes; times of calm progress, climax or decision. But
we feel that words fail us and there is a danger of our
applying to him the images which are appropriate to
our human spiritual life.

When the Son of God entered the world there
occurred that event our thought will never be able to
explore fully, and of which we were speaking: he who
now existed *was* as no other is.

Every creature is completely governed by God; each
belongs to him and exists through him. With Christ
all is different. The Logos has embraced all things, and
drawn them not only into his sphere of power, but also
into his sphere of being, into that realm where he says:
"I am who am". This is the absolute beginning. Between him and all creation lies nothingness. By becom-

ing man, the Son drew the creation which he had laid hold of right through this nothingness into the first beginning. There he performed an act of creation; not in the sense that there had been nothing and now something came into being; but in the sense that an existent being *was*, was drawn into God's existence, and emerged as something new.

In the midst of creation in its sinful state, a centre was born which the Son of God drew into his own being. It is there now—the starting-point of new life.

This starting-point cannot be explained in terms of this world, but its rays light up the whole world. From this point the Logos reaches out and takes hold of the world, bit by bit—or else the world shuts itself up against him, is thereby judged and falls back into darkness.